In Memory
of

All the young men from the villa
who lost their lives in the two
World Wars of the 20th Century

AND IN PARTICULAR

Private OWEN EMRYS WILLIAMS
14410986, 4th Bn., Welch Regiment
who died age 19
on 23 July 1944
Son of Thomas and Catherine E. Williams, of Morfa Nevin,
Caernarvonshire.
Remembered with honour
BANNEVILLE-LA-CAMPAGNE WAR CEMETERY

Commemorated in perpetuity by
Commonwealth War Graves Commission

Owen (Now Cae Bach) was a class mate of the author at Morfa Nefyn School

Acknowledgements

I wish to convey my thanks to the following people.

Gwenllian and Tony Jones (Rhiw.Com) who are always willing to share information and photographs.
Mr. M. Massarelli, Mrs. C. Evans and Mr. G. Morgan for the loan of a number of photographs.
Mrs. Gwerfyl Gregory for her assistance in re-producing a number of the old photographs.
Mrs. Aileen Jones for her help with the story of the San Demetrio.
Margaret Williams and her brother John for the loan of their father's photographs and for details of his life.
Dewi Evans for his personal recollection of his war-time experience.
Manon Williams for typing the original script and Geraint Roberts for reading through the final draft.
Gwasg Carreg Gwalch for their ever available help and support.

Profits from the sale of this book will be shared between the R.N.L.I. and the National Trust. The money to be spent on their respective local museums/information centres.

SOURCES

BOOKS

Eglwys M.C. Morfa Nefyn - John Owen
Cofiant y Parch. Edward James - O. L. Roberts
Packet to Ireland - M. Ellis Williams
Growing up among sailors - J. Ifor Davies
Coaches and coachmen of Lleyn - E. Kenrick
Mynd a dod ar Benrhyn Llŷn - E. J. Griffith
Silent Hunters - T. P. Zavas
U-Boat Adventurers - M. Wiggins
Twilight of the U-Boats - B. Edwards
The Dark Seas Remember - G. P. Phillips
Nightmare Convoy - P. Lund and H. Ludlam

INTERNET

Uboat.net
Uboatwaffe.net
britishmerchantnavy.co.uk
Cronab.demon.co.uk
Gordon Mumford.com
Ahoy-Mac's Web Log
Tower Hill Memorial
War Graves Commission

Part 1

Times Past

Morfa in 1850

The locality in 1850 was a windswept heathland with extensive patches of gorse, bracken and heather interspersed with numerous ponds and marshland. There were hardly any trees to be seen apart from small thorn bushes bent by the prevailing wind. The few trees in existence today were all planted during the last century to provide shade and shelter for the small farms like Cae Coch and Llwyn Gwalch and the larger houses such as Rhiwlas and Bodlondeb. Traces of the original landscape can still be seen but house building, land reclamation and improved farming have resulted in immense changes.

A comprehensive picture of Morfa Nefyn 150 years ago can be obtained from a study of the census returns for 1851. The village at that time was a very scattered rural community of 140 dwellings with a population of about 500 inhabitants. All properties had Welsh names apart from the group of three small cottages – Mount Pleasant. The name was probably conjured up by the estate, which owned them – Bryn Hyfryd would have been a much more sensible name in an all Welsh locality. Most of the dwellings in Morfa Nefyn were rented properties and the householders were tenants of one or the other of the estates of the landed gentry – Madryn, Nanhoron, Cefn Amwlch, Boduan and Glynllifon. Numerous houses which existed in 1850 have been demolished but a few of the senior residents in the village will be familiar with names such as Iwerddon, Tŷ Main, Cwt y Gêr, Ty'n y Mur. Some will also remember the terrace of six cottages which stood where the bungalow Ceiri in Lôn Terfyn now stands. They were on a slight slope with the highest cottage called Tŷ Uchaf, the lowest Tŷ Isaf and the one in the middle Tŷ Canol. The last remaining of these was put to various uses after it ceased to be inhabited – for a short period it was used as a Reading Room for the village and then as a workshop of one type or another.

There were two small terraces which were referred to as the Barracks. One of three houses (the ruins can still be seen) was off a small lane in Cefn Morfa between Cil and Fron Deg. The other six houses existed at the rear of the present chip shop. Barracks was a term used for shelters originally built for workmen who spent time away from home on some project or other and for whom daily travel was out of the question.

A number of today's houses have the same name as houses in 1850 but have no resemblance to the original structures. Vast improvements, alterations and extensions have been made over the years as at Ty'n Lôn and Bryn Cytun, and in some cases new larger houses have been built adjoining the old much smaller property of the same name. Erw and Erw Goch are good examples of the latter. Many houses have, of course, had their names changed and so it is rather difficult to determine how old they are and also impossible to accurately decide on their exact location.

Most of the dwellings in 1850 were small stone built structures and some are in existence today – Cae Coch, Bryn Bras, Cae'r Pwll, Pedair Llathan and many others. The exterior of these properties illustrate quite clearly the type of dwellings in which people lived during the middle part of the last century. It is interesting to note that these older properties were all built with a southerly or easterly aspect, with small windows in the front of the houses and very often none at the rear. The main reason for this was to take advantage of daylight particularly in the morning as they had very limited means of lighting up their homes. This also ensured as much warmth as possible for the residents.

The single storey houses would be rectangular in shape and would have one door, roughly in the centre of the front of the house. Flanking the door would be two little windows, again roughly symmetrical in size and position. The rubble stone walls had large boulders at their base and the roof in some cases would be thatched whilst others would be covered in small slates which would be the cheapest output of the North Wales quarries. The interior of these cottages has been described in many publications and I consider the extract below as the one giving the most accurate picture of the type of house in Morfa Nefyn in 1850.

> "As you enter through the door, the kitchen/living room is on one side, a small room with no ceiling between the floor and the roof. On one side of the door as you enter is a wooden partition, three feet wide and six feet high, to keep out the cold. On the other side as you go in there is a wooden partition running up to the roof with two doors in it, one vertically above the other. Through the lower door you enter the bedroom and this has a wooden ceiling which serves as a floor to the attic or croglofft above. To get to the croglofft you used a small ladder."

Some of the houses would be slightly larger with a full first floor, dormer windows in the roof and a small window in the gable end. A number of the houses would probably have their exterior walls limewashed.

Even the smallest cottage would have a large garden in which the tenants would grow their own vegetables. Some would have a strip of land adjoining the houses where hens and maybe other animals could be kept and nearly every property had a pigsty.

There were only two or three large houses in existence in 1850. The population of Morfa in 1850 was 590 made up of 252 males and 338 females. Of this total only 42 people were over the age of 65 whereas 258 were under the age of 18. Every inhabitant (apart from 3) had been born in Wales, the vast majority of them within a 10 mile radius of Morfa Nefyn.

In 1850 there were only 7 uninhabited houses whereas today there are well over 100 so-called 2nd homes which are empty most of the year. Their owners either occupy them or let them during the holiday season. Another interesting fact is that in 1850 only 4 people (2 men, 2 women) lived on their own compared with 95 (76 women, 19 men) at the present time.

Being an isolated rural, coastal community it was only natural that most people made a living in occupations dependant on both the land and the sea. Within the confines of Morfa there were 20 small farms which varied in size from Bryn Bach (4 acres), Erw Goch (5 acres) to Cae Coch (24 acres) and Bryn Cytun (24 acres). The following figures of the number employed in various categories clearly illustrate this land/sea dependency.

Farmers	20	Mariners	45
Agricultural labourers	29	Ship builders	4
		Ship's carpenters	19
		Fishermen	2
		Tide waiter and Boatman	2

A community like Morfa Nefyn in the 1850s before the advent of mass production required the services of a variety of craftsmen and women and the following occupations were to be found.

Dress maker	5	Tailor	2
Clock maker	1	Weaver	1
Slater	5	Glazier	1
Stone Mason	3	idwife	1
Carrier	3	Joiner	2
Mantua Maker	1	Butcher	1
		Blacksmith	1

Another interesting category which appears in the returns is the occupation of House Servant. In this day and age it is difficult to understand how in a community of small cottages and small farms there were 23 House Servants employed. They worked on some of the small farms and were also employed by the Master Mariners who lived in the village. A number of them were young girls who probably worked long hours for hardly any wages, but food and shelter would have been provided. Other interesting entries in the 1851 census returns is the 3 women and 1 man who are referred to as paupers. In one dwelling the Head of the Family was a 10 year old boy called Robert Hughes and the other occupant is his brother Thomas. They were obviously orphaned children and their home was a house somewhere near the present Glanrafon Terrace.

Another point of interest is that in 1851, 71 people lived in Porthdinllaen, a family of 6 in Hen Blas and 17 people in Bwlch which made a total of 94 living on the beach.

Typical 19th Century cottage known as Lôn Las. It was my mother's home during her childhood.

The Village Takes Shape

The two world wars of the last century act as dividing lines between 3 distinct periods in the growth of the village.

1850 – WORLD WAR I

In this period a large number of very substantial well-built properties were erected ranging from terraced and semi-detached houses to large detached dwellings. The latter were built by men who were connected in one way or another with shipping either as master mariners, ship builders or owners. A number of the houses were very similar to each other in design which makes one think that the owners were anxious to have as fine a house as their neighbour down the road.

An interesting local story concerns the building of one of the houses namely Llys Olwen. A certain Capt. Lloyd had purchased a plot of land to build a house on. Before departing on a lengthy voyage he gave detailed instructions to his wife to have a large detached house built. Mrs. Lloyd who had a mind of her own, decided to change the plans and build two semi-detached houses on the site as a surprise for her husband. When her husband returned, however, he was furious and immediately arranged for the original detached house to be built in the same field. This was done giving satisfaction to Capt. Lloyd who named the house after his ship "Dauntless". Dauntless House is now known as Llys Olwen and the similarity between it and the two adjoining houses is very obvious.

In 1850 there were no places of worship in Morfa Nefyn but the next 25 years saw the establishment of 3 chapels and the church. Prior to this people had walked to Nefyn to attend services but the growing interest in religious worship and the growth of the village led to a demand for places of worship within the confines of Morfa Nefyn itself. The non-conformist movement with its rigid denominational divides resulted in three chapels being established in the village – Methodist, Baptist and Congregational with accommodation for more worshipers than the village would ever need. The seating capacity of the three buildings were as follows:-

Moriah – 500	Tabernacl – 260	Caersalem – 160

The local school was also built before the onset of the 1st World War.

The growth of the village resulted in more and more retail outlets being established and a directory of 1883 names the following

Bakers and Flour Dealers	-	Ellis Griffiths
		Jane Jones
		Winifred Jones
		Owen Owen
Boot and Shoe Makers	-	William Roberts
		John Williams
		David Williams
Butchers	-	William Jones

China, Glass & Earthenware Dealers	-	Griffith Thomas
Post Office	-	David Davies
Groceries and Tea Dealers	-	Ellis Griffiths
		Griffith Jones
		Winifred Jones
		Owen Owen
		Hugh Parry
Linen Drapers	-	David Davies
		Mary Pritchard

Another milestone in this period was the development of telegraphic communication across the Irish Sea by means of underwater cables. Cables were laid from Aber Geirch in 1892 and 1898 to Newcastle which is just north of Dublin and to a small town called Howth on the Irish coast.

In the early years the system was manually operated and a depot had to be established to house the machinery, switchboard etc. To begin with this was based at Plas Tirion which was rented from the owner Griffith Owen who had built the property in 1884. The depot was later moved across the road to a large annexe to the house Ashdene (now Plas Madryn) which had been built by Mr. Wales the first superintendent of the telegraph office.

A number of men were employed at the office and they moved to live locally with their families. Gradually, however, the need for the system to be operated manually came to an end and a new automatic station was opened in 1938 in the centre of the village – this has also long been redundant and the building is now a private house.

1918-1940

In the aftermath of the 1st World War the villagers following public meetings decided to construct a War Memorial and also to build a Village Hall. All the money was raised locally for both these ventures. The Village Hall, on the same site as the present Community Centre, was opened in 1921 and the War Memorial was unveiled in 1923.

More houses were built by local people particularly in the part of the village to the west of Cae Coch. Also built in this period were the Linksway Hotel, the present Golf Club and the Coastguard houses.

Shops were established at strategic locations throughout the village and the list below is of those in existence in the 1930s.

Glanrafon	- grocery
Mrs. Whitfield	- mall grocery
Arddwen	- butchers
Pantlon	- butcher then grocery
Newlands	- newsagent/confectioners
Park Stores	- ronmongers/grocers/butcher
Post Office	
Rhiwlas	- small wooden shop opposite P.O.
Penrhos	- small grocery
Beach	- open during holiday season

Jones Terrace	- small sweet shop
William Hughes	- greengrocers
William Jones	- butcher
Chip Shop	
Watchmaker	
Lloyd's	- grocers
Glasgoed	- shoe shop
Penrorsedd	- greengrocer
D. Owen	- small wooden shop on Nefyn road later became a barber shop

During this period there were also far more door to door deliveries made. Bread was delivered daily – Mr. Akers baked in the building behind his house Gwynfor and delivered by means of a small handcart. There were three farms selling milk and delivering by pony and trap and greengrocery rounds were regularly made particularly in the summer months. Another important weekly delivery was paraffin, again by means of a small handcart – it was a very important source of cooking and lighting in the days prior to electricity coming to the village – I still have my oil delivered by the same firm.

POST WAR PERIOD

During the post war period there have been tremendous changes in Morfa Nefyn as in every other community throughout the country. A very significant change has been in the development of speculative house building resulting in housing estates in various parts of the village. Planning was given for all these developments at a time when there was no real housing need in the area – the result is that a significant number of these dwellings (over 50%) are second homes occupied for only about 2 months a year.

At the time of writing, the largest building ever built in Morfa Nefyn is nearing completion, specifically as holiday accommodation. I have no comment to make about the impact of this development but I do hope that the people responsible will have the good sense and courtesy to give the place a Welsh name (preferably one that English people can pronounce).

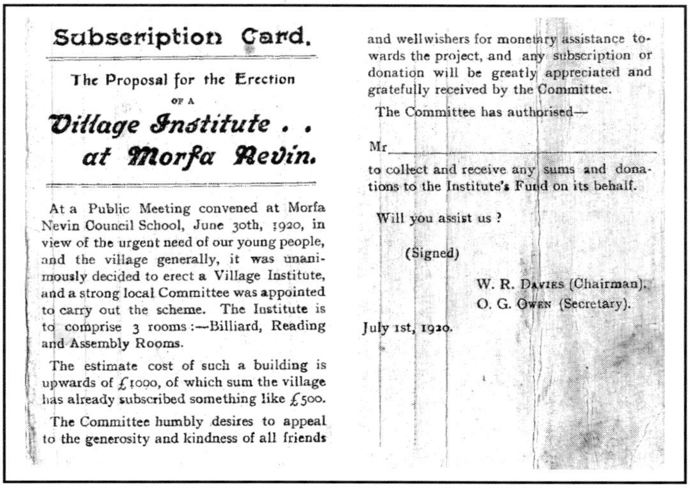

Subscription Card.

The Proposal for the Erection of a

Village Institute . . at Morfa Nevin.

At a Public Meeting convened at Morfa Nevin Council School, June 30th, 1920, in view of the urgent need of our young people, and the village generally, it was unanimously decided to erect a Village Institute, and a strong local Committee was appointed to carry out the scheme. The Institute is to comprise 3 rooms:—Billiard, Reading and Assembly Rooms.

The estimate cost of such a building is upwards of £1000, of which sum the village has already subscribed something like £500.

The Committee humbly desires to appeal to the generosity and kindness of all friends and wellwishers for monetary assistance towards the project, and any subscription or donation will be greatly appreciated and gratefully received by the Committee.

The Committee has authorised—

Mr____________________

to collect and receive any sums and donations to the Institute's Fund on its behalf.

Will you assist us?

(Signed)

W. R. Davies (Chairman).
O. G. Owen (Secretary).

July 1st, 1920.

Morfa in the 1920s
The long building in the centre was the Village Hall

A quiet road to the beach.

Open spaces prior to housing estates

Education

There was no school in Morfa during the 19th century but with the growth of non-conformist religion some informal education was carried out by the various denominations. Prior to the erection of places of worship numerous children were taught to read the Bible etc. in the houses of a few concerned local people. Methodists in the village had organised religious schools at houses such as Tyn y Coed, Cae'r Pwll and Tan y Bryn since the beginning of the century and by 1850 there was a well organised Sunday school being held at Bryngoleu. A voluntary day school was also held here for a time with the pupils being instructed by a Mr. John Peter. A gentleman by the name of Roland Williams held a Sunday school in his house on the beach for many years. He was a weaver by trade and a devout Baptist and many youngsters learnt to read Welsh following attendance at his house. Schools were established in Nevin (1861) and Edern (1846) and a few youngsters from Morfa used to attend these schools. With the coming of compulsory education in the 1870s all children from the village went to school at either Nefyn or Edern. They walked to school and the pattern was for those living west of Cae Coch to go to Edern and those on the other side of the village to attend at Nefyn. A very small privileged number were sent by their parents to continue their education in the grammar school at Pwllheli but not until after the First World War did attendance at the latter become more common place. Prior to a school being established in Morfa, a couple of attempts were also made to run some form of private schooling particularly for girls. During the latter years of the 19th century, Mrs. Jones, the landlady of the Tŷ Coch Inn at Porthdinllaen, held classes for young girls where she taught them reading and simple arithmetic together with some needlework and music. Needlework lessons involved the completion of samplers which also assisted the girls in learning the alphabet.

In the early years of the last century a private school was established at Plas Tirion again mainly for girls. The school was the brainchild of Mrs. Laurence Hart who had come to live in Morfa with her family. The Hart family originated from Birmingham and Mr. J. Lawrence Hart was a Landscape Artist of some repute. This fact, together with poor health probably were the reasons why the family moved to Morfa Nefyn. Mr. Hart died on October 23rd 1907 at the age of 57.

The prospectus for this establishment (see extract) gives the impression that it was a large school with excellent facilities and highly qualified staff. The venture (1904 – 1907) was not an outstanding success – there was very little request for boarding places and local people preferred to send their children to the state schools in Nefyn and Edern.

This was the pattern until 1908 when Morfa Nefyn school was opened on November 2nd with 60 pupils and two teachers. The school was built of corrugated iron on a wooden structure and always painted red. There were 2 classrooms, 2 cloakrooms with 2 stone built shelters and toilets at the rear of the playground and a small coal shed near the road. A bell hung outside near the main entrance which would be rung by means of a long pole with a hook on the end of it. Ringing the bell to herald the start of the school day was a great honour for a young lad. Heating was provided by large coal fired stoves in each classroom and although they burnt brightly their efficiency on very cold days was questionable.

Until 1968–69 pupils were taught in Morfa school until they were 10 years old and then went to Nefyn where they stayed until they left school or transferred after 1 year (following an examination) to the Grammar School at Pwllheli.

Since 1969 pupils have transferred to Nefyn at 8 years old and with the onset of comprehensive education parents now have the choice of sending children to secondary schools at either Pwllheli or Botwnnog and Nefyn has long since ceased to be an all age school.

The new school at Morfa was opened in 1981 and the present headmistress is the ninth lady to have held the post. As the list that follows shows, Elisabeth Roberts was in charge for 28 years which is much longer than any of her predecessors.

1908	Miss Grace Alice Roberts	7 years
1915	Miss Mary Jones	2 years
1917	Miss Jennie Ryle Davies	1 year
1918	Miss Euronwy Roberts	3 years
1921	Miss Enid Catherine Owen	17 years
1938	Miss Edith Evans	18 years
1956	Miss Hannah A. Griffith	16 years
1972	Mrs. Elisabeth Roberts	28 years
2000	Mrs. Gwennan Jones	

She was also the first married woman to have held the post and I think she is the only ex pupil of the school to become its headmistress.

Morfa school has always had a reputation for being a good school and it is pleasing to note that the present headmistress and her assistant Mrs. Nia Williams have maintained this excellent tradition. The latest report on the school following a recent inspection makes very pleasing reading.

"Pupil standards in lessons are much higher than the targets set by the Assembly Government for the whole of Wales"

"The school provides a high quality of educational provision and standards."

The village owes a considerable debt to these two ladies and to all the other ladies who have taught at Morfa throughout the years.

Morfa Nevin College . . .

FOR GIRLS,

With Boys' Preparatory Forms,

MORFA NEVIN-ON-THE-SEA,

NORTH WALES.

Principals:

Mrs. LAURENCE HART

AND

Miss F. LAURENCE HART.

Head Mistress:

Miss MARY THOMAS B.A.,

Staff of Highly Certificated Teachers and Non-Resident Professors.

MORFA NEVIN.

Morfa Nevin is one of the most healthy watering-places, situated in the beautiful Bay of Carnarvon. It has a fine beach of sand, magnificent senery, affording unlimited woodland, moorland, and cliff walks. Owing to its dry and bracing climate and singularly mild winters, it is particularly beneficial to delicate girls. There is excellent bathing free from danger at all times.

* * *

THE COLLEGE stands in its own grounds, facing South, and is within seven minutes walk of the sea. It is spacious and well appointed. Large and airy class-rooms; Sunny Dormitories (single beds). The health and comfort of the entire Household are under the personal supervision of Principals, who endeavour to combine the comforts of Home Life, with the advantages of school discipline.

DIETARY. Nutritious, varied, and unlimited. All details which tend to develop the physical nature and establish a good physique are considered as matters of supreme importance.

* * *

OUT DOOR SPORTS are encouraged, as far as considered beneficial for girls, by modern medical authority. These include Swimming (which is taught by Trained Teacher), Cycling, Tennis, and Hockey. There is also a Botanical Cycling Club in connection with the Higher Forms.

* * *

THE PUPILS RECEIVE Christian training, and are taught to develop habits of observation and usefulness, and to foster a spirit of reverence for all that is noble and beautiful. The utmost care and attention is devoted to their ladylike behaviour and deportment at all times. If desired, they may also be trained in light domestic duties, and cooking.

Pupils at Plas Tirion – early last century

Pupils – Circa 1910

*Circa 1929-30. The teacher (Miss Parry) became Mrs. Jones (Chemist, Nefyn)
I was pleased to learn she recently celebrated her 100th birthday*

Early 1930s

Look carefully – they are all a little older in the photograph below

Can you spot a future headmistress

The pupils in both photographs are now adults

Mrs. Roberts and Miss Ann Hughes at the opening of the new school

Mrs. Elizabeth Roberts retirement surprise From T.V. chef Dudley

Religious Worship

BAPTIST - CAERSALEM

Before the chapel was built people had been meeting and worshipping in numerous houses in the village, amongst them Terfyn, Cae Coch and Bryn Bach and a Sunday school was regularly held in the house of a local weaver called Rowland Williams. He had come to live in Morfa Nefyn when he married Mary Williams, the daughter of Cae Coch, a small farm in the centre of the village. For a short time they lived in a thatched cottage in the village before moving to another small cottage on the beach about half-way between Bwlch and Hen Blas. It was while living here that Rowland came to realise that the many children who lived at Porthdinllaen had no opportunity to receive any formal education or religious instruction. He encouraged them to attend a Sunday School which he established in his own house in 1833 in very cramped conditions and he did his best in teaching them himself. The school became extremely popular with regular attendance being maintained until an unfortunate epidemic struck the Williams household. Rowland was forced to close the school when two of his own eight children died as a result of the fever.

In 1848, however, the school re-opened in property at the rear of and belonging to the large house (Tŷ Newydd) on the beach at Bwlch. The property known as Y Gegin (The Kitchen) became extremely important not only as a Sunday School for young children but also as a meeting place for adults. It was the forerunner of the local Baptist Chapel in Morfa Nefyn and Rolant Williams can really be looked upon as one of the prime movers in establishing the movement locally and for many years the chapel was referred to as Caersalem, Porthdinllaen.

It very soon became obvious that a central place of worship was required as the houses were too small to accommodate everyone.

It was decided to build a chapel in the centre of the village and an approach was made to the owner of the land, Mr. John Charles Jones, who agreed to sell a plot 15 yards x 27 yards for £52-10-0 (I have also seen £30 quoted as the price paid). Stones for the erection of the chapel were carried by horse and cart from the small cove at Bryn Gwydd, Edern and from the granite quarries at Nefyn. Local farmers performed this task free of charge among them being:-

Robert Williams	Porthdinllaen
William Williams	Ty'n Llan
Robert Jones	Cae Glas
Hugh Parry	Terfyn
John Jones	Erw
Thomas Williams	Cae Coch

The chapel was completed towards the end of 1853 and the first trustees were appointed in January 1854. They were:

Hugh Parry	Terfyn
Griffith Jones	Pwllheli (Timber Merchant)
Thomas Williams	Penrhos
Hugh Jones	Waen
William Evans	Bwlch (Master Mariner)

There were 37 members to begin with but this more than doubled in less than 10 years and the list of members for 1854 and 1862 (following pages) illustrate this fact. A considerable number of the residents of Porthdinllaen were members and perhaps this was the reason why the chapel was for many years referred to as Caersalem, Porthdinllaen.

It is interesting to note the contributions made by members for the upkeep of the movement in 1862 and also donations made by villagers towards the renovation of the chapel in 1896. Collectors who went from door to door requesting contributions for the renovation carried with them a note written in English appealing for donations. A copy of this well written letter follows:-

CAERSALEM
BAPTIST CHAPEL
MORFA NEVIN

Dear Sir or Madam,

The members of the above church have decided to build a new chapel as soon as circumstances will permit. Our present chapel is old, having been built in the year 1850 and also it is too small for the congregation assembling therein. For a small church of 70 members this undertaking, which we are obliged to take, is heavy, therefore we appeal to all Christian friends for help; and we do so in full confidence because in so doing you will help to bear another's burdens and so "fulfil the law of Christ".

Contributions in money will be most gratefully received and acknowledged either by the bearer of this book or any of the undersigned.

We remain, dear Sir or Madam

Most respectfully yours,

William Jones, Glanrafon House, Treasurer
John Jones, Tanyparc Shop, Secretary
Daniel Jones, Terfyn, Deacon

The chapel has had many resident ministers over the years and it was a shared ministry with the chapel at Nefyn. Below is a list of those who have held the position.

Thomas Hughes	1854-1854
Lewis Roberts	1854-1856
Thomas Griffith	1856-1863
Stephen Thomas	1863-1868
Nathaniel Davies	1868-1880
Emmanuel Jones	1880-1889
D. H. Hughes	1889-1893
No minister for some years	
D. Wyre Lewis	1900-1910
Idris Thomas	1914-1919
D. R. Owen	1921-1937
W. H. Rowlands	1939-1948
Aneurin Davies	1949-1954
Bryn Jones	1955-1956
Idris Williams	1957-1965
O. J. Hughes	1965-1970s

In addition to resident ministers it was customary throughout the years for visiting clergy to come and preach at the chapel on Sundays and it is interesting to note how much they were paid in 1855.

Hugh Hughes	Llanllyfni	2.6
Edward James		1.0
David Thomas		2.6
William Jones	Sarn	2.0
Hugh Howell		2.0
Moses Roberts	Llangernyw	6.0
Robert Jones	Llanllyfni	6.0
John Morgans	Caernarfon	2.0
William Lewis		2.0
John Williams	Caernarfon	2.0

By the beginning of this century regular Sunday attendance at the chapel rarely reached double figures and despite the valiant efforts of a few stalwarts the chapel was forced to close its doors for the last time in November 2003.

Names of original members Caersalem Porthdinllaen – October 16th 1854

1. Thomas Hughes
2. Rowland Williams
3. Thomas Williams
4. David Williams
5. Griffith Williams
6. Owen Jones Terfyn
7. Humphrey Williams
8. John Jones Erw
9. Ebenezer Roberts
10. Hugh Parry
11. Watkin Williams Porthdinllaen
12. Owen Williams Porthdinllaen
13. Hugh Jones Waen
14. John Herbert Porthdinllaen
15. Hugh Thomas
16. Jane Roberts, Terfyn
17. Sara Evans
18. Mary Williams Penrhos
19. Ellen Williams Penrhos
20. Jane Griffith
21. Elin Jones Erw
22. Margaret Williams Penrhos
23. Jane Williams Tudweiliog
24. Ann Williams Erw
25. Elizabeth Jones Pedair Llathen
26. Margaret Foulkes Porthdinllaen
27. Laura Williams
28. Mary Parry
29. Ellen Jones Bwlch
30. Laura Roberts
31. Mary Griffiths
32. Jane Williams
33. Jane Hughes
34. Mary Williams Porthdinllaen
35. Margaret Hughes
36. Gwen Williams
37. Catherine Thomas

Members Contributions Caersalem 1862

1.	Rowland Williams	1-8
2.	Thomas Williams	5-0
3.	David Williams	1-9
4.	Griffith Williams	2
5.	John Jones Erw	2-0
6.	Ebenezer Roberts	2-6
7.	Hugh Parry	1-8
8.	Watkin Williams	1-5
9.	Hugh Jones	11
10.	John Herbert	
11.	Hugh Thomas	11
12.	John Williams	2-0
13.	William Williams	
14.	Henry Roberts Plas Newydd	£1-3-0
15.	Nehemiah Bracegirdle	5-0
16.	Humphrey Williams	1-10
17.	Hugh Hughes	
18.	John Williams	1-3
19.	William Williams	
20.	Robert Williams	1-6
21.	Thomas Williams	1-0
22.	Jeremiah Jones	4
23.	Griffith Jones	
24.	David Parry	3-0
25.	Hugh Jones	
26.	Robert Evans	2-6
27.	Daniel Williams	
28.	William Parry	2-6
29.	Robert Pritchard	7
30.	Henry Roberts	10
31.	Mary Williams	
32.	Ellen Williams	4-0
33.	Jane Griffith	1
34.	Ellen Jones Erw	1-10
35.	Margaret Williams	10
36.	Elizabeth Jones	
37.	Jane Williams	11
38.	Margaret Foulkes	6
39.	Ellen Jones Pen y Bryn	5
40.	Laura Roberts	1-6
41.	Mary Griffiths	4
42.	Jane Williams	5
43.	Jane Hughes	7
44.	Mary Williams	
45.	Jane Herbert	9
46.	Catherine Roberts	
47.	Ann Roberts	9
48.	Jane Williams	1-2
49.	Elizabeth Jones Henborth	7
50.	Jane Bracegirdle	6
51.	Elizabeth Jones Pantrorsedd	3
52.	Margaret Roberts Penybryn	2
53.	Sydney Hughes	6
54.	Margaret Roberts	8
55.	Catherine Pritchard	6
56.	Ann Jones Erw	6
57.	Martha Jones	5
58.	Laura Williams	3-0
59.	Gwen Williams	9
60.	Elizabeth Williams Bryn Bach	3
61.	Mary Jones	7
62.	Elizabeth Williams Pen Palmant	2
63.	Jane Jones Storehouse	2
64.	Mary Williams Penrhos	4
65.	Catherine Evans	7
66.	Margaret Jones	6
67.	Sara Parry	1-4
68.	Mary Jones	3
69.	Hannah Jones	
70.	Ann Jones Henborth	2
71.	Jane Williams Henblas	8
72.	Ann Jones, Edern	1-4
73.	Mary Jones	4
		£4-14-8

Caersalem

a adgyweiriwyd yn y flwyddyn 1896

	Talwyd I
Griffith Jones Contractor	£92-12-0
William Owen, Painter	£ 7-10-0
Mân gostau	£ 8-7-6
Cyfanswm	£111-9-6

Rhoddion at gostau'r adgyweirio

Hugh Roberts	Tŷ Capel	£ 7-10-0
Catherine Parry	Waen	5-10-0
Ann Herbert	Bodawen	4-0-0
Henry Parry	Waen	3-10-0
Jane Jones	Henblas	3-3-0
Ann Jones	Erw	3-2-6
William Jones	Bwlch	1-13-9
William J. Parry	Waen	3-0-0
Robert Thomas	Cae Coch	1-16-0
Hugh Williams	Pen Rhos	1-11-6
John Jones	Erw	1-0-0
Sarah Parry	Penrallt	1-7-0
R. & C. Thomas	Bryn raur	1-6-0
D. Morris Jones	Penrhos	1-5-0
Daniel Jones	Frondeg	1-2-3
Mary Jones	Penrhos	1-1-9
William Owen		1-0-0
Mary Jones	Plas Newydd	10-0
Eliza Jones	Glan Noddfa	5-0
Eliza Williams	Penrhos	4-0
Catherine Hunt	Henborth	10-0
Margery Evans	Tŷ Gwyn	3-11-0
Robert Williams	Penrallt	1-1-0
Eliza Jones	Henborth	10-6
Owen Jones	Chemist Nefyn	12-0
Cyngerdd Nefyn		12-0
R Roberts	Nefyn	1-0-0
Evan Williams	Nefyn	10-0
Ann Herbert		5-0
Jane Jones		2-6
O arian y Weinidogaeth		10-10-3
Gan y gymanfa		40-0-0
T. Thomas		5-0
Sydney Owen		10-0
William Jones		1-0-0
		£105-5-3

Y cyfarfod agoriadol	2-3-3 ½
Eistedd leoedd	2-14-3
Arian y Weinidogaeth	1-6-9
	£111-9-6

Casgliadau

Gan yr Eglwys	3-16-6
Yn y cyfarfod	3-15-3
	£ 7-11-9

Taliadau

I: Mr. Edwards Pwllheli	£ 1-0-0
Mr. Williams, Y Rhos	1-14-0
Mr. Jones, Llanelli	2-4-0
Mrs. Griffith am lanhau'r capel (M.C.)	2-6
Car John Hughes	6-0
Modulator	2-0
	£5-8-6

Dyled ar y capel 1897	£36-00

Caersalem Chapel

An adult Sunday School Class – the tutor was John Jones, Park Stores (seated).

Deacons at Caersalem Circa 1950.

CONGREGATIONAL – TABERNACL

The Congregational chapel was completed and opened in 1862 with 40 members. At the outset it was run as a branch of the chapel at Nefyn but this arrangement ceased in 1899 when Morfa and Penniel Chapel at Ceidio combined as one unit.

The chapel, which was built by Thomas Griffith of Edern, cost £391-17 and the architect was Joseph Morris of Madryn. One of the most prominent of the original members was William Griffith Tan y Parc who became the first treasurer of the chapel. It was he who approached Sir Love Jones Parry, Madryn and requested the lease on a plot of land in the village. The squire promised a lease for a thousand years but eventually the land was given to the movement free of charge – "tra rhed y dŵr" – a Welsh way of saying in perpetuity.

In 1900 the chapel was renovated and an extension built to house the Sunday school. Donations were more than adequate to cover the cost of the work done - £395. Two donations of note made earlier in the last century was the gift of two houses (Adenfa and Siop Pantlon) to the chapel by the late Mrs. Roberts, Ardwyn and £100 by the late Mrs. Col. Hughes, Gwynfor.

Resident ministers at the chapel have been

W. Williams	1862-1866
R. M. Roberts	1870-1872
Edward James	1872-1897
W. D. Evans	1899-1900
R. W. Davies	1901-1903
E. T. Evans	1904-1922
J. A. Morgan	1925-1959

No minister was appointed after the death of the Rev. Morgan and the chapel once again united with Nefyn. The membership was 60 in 1959 but continued to decrease in the next decade and this coupled with the expense of maintaining a large building sadly resulted in the chapel closing. It is now a plumber's workshop and store.

One of the most prominent of the numerous fine ministers who have served the chapel over the years was the Rev. Edward James who came to the village in 1872 and remained here until his death in 1904. He was renowned throughout the country as a very fine preacher and as a result he was in great demand at preaching festivals etc. and everyone referred to him affectionately as James Nefyn. He was a minister at Llanaelhaearn when he received a letter dated July 10th 1872 inviting him to become the minister in charge of the Congregational chapels at Nefyn and Morfa Nefyn. The letter in Welsh which follows clearly outlines the terms of the appointment with a salary of £50 per annum.

"At y Parch. Edward James"

Annwyl Syr,

Yr ydym ni sydd an henwau isod, dros y ddwy eglwys Gynulleidfaol neu annibynnol a ymgyferfydd yn Soar, Nefyn, a'r Tabernacl, Morfa, yn ein hymddifadrwydd o'n diweddar anwyl weinidog, Mr. Roberts, ar ol dwys ystyriaeth, wedi eich dewis chwi yn weinidog i bregethu yr Efengyl i ni, yn nghyda gwahanol ac amrywiol ranau gwaith yr Arglwydd yn ein plith, yn ol rheol neu drefn Annibyniaeth, yr hyn a gredir genym sydd yn unol â'r Testament Newydd. Am y cyfryw wasanaeth yr ydym yn addaw i chwi yn ol £30 y flwyddyn oddiwrth eglwys Soar, Nefyn, ac ugain punt (£20) y flwyddyn oddiwrth eglwys y Tabernacl, Morfa, felly yn gwneyd y cyfanswm yn £50 y flwyddyn. Yn mhellach, yr ydym yn addaw i chwi un mis yn y flwyddyn, neu, dyweder, bedwar Sabbath, at eich rhyddid eich hun, ac i'r ddwy chwaer eglwys fod yn atebol am wasanaeth y cyfryw fis. Os byddwch yn ewyllysio newid neu alw am weinidog neu bregethwr i ddyfod i wasanaethu yn eich lle rywbryd (ond y mis a nodwyd at eich rhyddid eich hun), dysgwylir i chwi fod yn gyfrifol am ei lety a'i wasanaeth. Hefyd, dysgwylir cael neu roddi 6 mis o rybudd cyn dadgysylltiad oddiwrth y gweinidog i'r eglwysi, ar un modd 6 mis oddiwrth yr eglwysi i'r gweinidog. Ein dymuniad yw, heb ymhelaethu, y bydd i chwi gydsynio â'n cais, ac y bydd y Pen Bugail yn goruchlywodraethu yr ymdrafodaeth i fod yn lles i'r achos, ac yn ogoniant iddo Ei Hun. Dysgwylir atebiad mor fuan ag y bydd yn gyfleus.

Nefyn	Morfa
JOHN ELIAS	HUGH JONES
WILLIAM OWEN	JOHN WILLIAMS
WILLIAM ROBERTS	JOHN JONES
JOSEPH DAVIES	HENRY PARRY

Nefyn, Gorphenhaf 10fed, 1872

Edward James and his family moved here in August 1872 to a house somewhere on the Nefyn road. In 1884 they moved to the small cottage Llwyn y Gwalch where his descendants resided until the last decade. His eldest son Edward Ambrose James for many years had a small drapers shop on the site now occupied by Claremont Garage.

The Rev. James's ministry at Morfa Nefyn was most successful and attendance at services, and chapel membership increased twofold under his guidance. He also managed to clear the debt of £232 which had remained from 1862. Even after his retirement in 1897 he remained as a deacon in the chapel until his death on Tuesday December 21st 1904. A very large crowd attended his funeral at Nefyn and a memorial service addressed by the Rev. O. L. Roberts, Liverpool was held at Morfa Nefyn on December 27th.

Llwyn Gwalch – The James Family home

Rev. Edward James

Rev. J. A. Morgan

METHODIST – MORIAH

The Methodist movement in Morfa Nefyn began early in the 19th century and it is worth recording developments prior to 1850. The man responsible for starting it all was William Robert Dafydd who lived at Tynycoed, Cefn Morfa. One Sunday in 1810 he decided to persuade a group of young children from the locality to attend a Sunday school in his cowshed. He sat them on stools and baskets in the stalls, narrating biblical stories to them and teaching them the alphabet by chalking letters on stone and bits of wood. Later he had the use of short pamphlets to assist in his story telling. The school was a great success and within a very short time the cowshed was too small and the school was moved to the two houses at Llainfadryn. Unfortunately William Robert Dafydd was drowned while fishing off Nefyn point.

In 1815 a gentleman by the name of John Thomas had built a large house called Tan y Bryn on the other side of the village and he allowed the school to be held on the premises. More and more pupils attended and the school was moved for a time to the Tithe Barn situated on the Nefyn Road not far from the vicarage. From there it moved to Caerpwll which was too small from the outset and many other houses in that locality were also used. The next move was to Bryngoleu (opposite the present chapel) where in those days there were six cottages (the Barracks) in two rows of three. The new school building was erected between the two rows and it was big enough to accommodate all the pupils which by this time numbered over 100. Numerous local people acted as teachers and the emphasis was on biblical teaching and learning to read. At one stage the building was also used as a day school which children attended voluntarily to be taught by an ex-sailor called John Peter.

This building which was erected in 1824 continued to be used until the first chapel was built in 1853-54 roughly opposite where the present chapel stands (a modern bungalow now occupies the site). The old chapel was a simple square building which very soon proved to be too small for the congregation. It was extended in 1857 when a chapel house was also built and in 1860 a gallery was constructed. In 1855 there were 60 worshipers which rapidly grew to 93 in 1859, 150 in 1861, 172 in 1864 and about 260 by 1880 by which time the building was far too small and plans were prepared for the erection of a new chapel. A small field opposite was bought for £60 from Capt. Robert Davies, Erw Goch and the present Moriah Chapel was opened on 25th May 1882. Prior to the new chapel being ready the congregation met in a temporary wooden building adjacent to the site.

Moriah cost nearly £2,000 to build and details of the expenditure is listed. The members themselves contributed over half of the cost and substantial amounts were donated by residents who by now were relatively wealthy many having made their money by being shareholders, builders or captains of sailing ships which at that period were in their heyday. The list of the donations made illustrate this fact.

Ministers who have served the movement diligently throughout the years are listed below:-

Evan Williams	1857 – 1889
Robert Roberts	1889 – 1893
Griffith Parri Hughes	1894 – 1926
D. R. Lewis	1928 – 1935
Caradog Rowlands	1936 – 1956
Edryd Edwards	1951 – 1964
T. Arthur Pritchard	1967 – 1974
Emrys W. Thomas	1975 – 1985
R. O. Roberts	1986 –

During the 20th century considerable improvements were made to the chapel and a great deal of money spent. In 1921 a sum of £525 was spent to light the building by means of electricity and in later years a system of central heating was introduced. In 1931 a house was built for the minister – Awelon on Lôn Penrhos which cost £1,200.

The Methodist movement was always the most dominant in the village and it remains so although present membership is far less than the 260 who subscribed to the chapel towards the end of the 19th century.

There are many reasons for the decline in religious worship and chapel attendance during the last 50 years and the chapels themselves must shoulder some of the blame for this. Nevertheless one should never forget the contribution they have made towards ensuring the survival of the Welsh language and to the religious, cultural and social life of the village – the tremendous efforts of the founder members were not in vain.

Moriah Chapel

Capel Moriah – agorwyd 25ain o Fai 1882
TALIADAU

Talwyd i:	£ s c
William Jones, Contractor	1510-0-0
Robert Jones, Mason am waliau, ystabl etc.	75-10-0
Robert Davies, Erw Goch am y tir	60-0-0
O. M. Roberts, yr Architect	55-1-6
William Jones am y Capel coed	35-0-0
Jane Jones, Ironmonger, Nevin am Lampau etc.	18-10-0
David Davies, Emporium, am y carpedau etc.	15-12-0
Breese Jones & Casson am y Gweithredoedd	12-0-0
William Jones, am Gadeiriau a Bwrdd i'r Set Fawr	10-0-0
Hugh Williams, Edeyrn am y Clock	6-0-0
Evan Williams, Gof. Nevin am Gate haiarn	3-10-6
Mary Pritchard, Shop am Garpedau, Oil cloth etc.	3-3-0
Catherine Jones, Brynyraur am wasanaeth ei thy	2-0-0
Robert Williams, Auctioneer am werthu tir yr Hen Gapal	2-2-0
Robert Owen, Pwllheli, am Lyfrau Casglu, Llyfrau Hymnau Tonau etc.	5-0-0
William Griffith, Caernarvon am Envelopes	2-1-0
John Griffith, Nevin etc.	-19-6
William Thomas, Nevin am osod y carpedau etc.	18-0
Jane Jones, Cefngoleu am lanhau	1-10-0
Rowland Williams am lanhau y lampau etc.	10-0
Am fatiau o flaen y Set Fawr	5-6
Costau teithio er cwblhau y Gweithredoedd	8-0
I'r "Herald Gymraeg" am adverteisio am Tenders	1- 2-6
I'r "Genedl Gymreig" etc.	18-0
William Roberts, Shopymaes, am Feibl ar y Set Fawr	5-6
Am Bill Stamps	8-10
R. W. Thomas, Nefyn am Tapes etc at y Carpedau	4-6
Thomas Rowlands, am gario gro o flaen y capel	7-6
Am gario Parselau ar wahanol adegau	6-4
Griffith Jones, Joiner am waith	12-0
Eto am waith – repairs	1-1-0
Gwen Jones am Oil, Canwyllau etc.	12-0
Fire Insurance	1-6-6
Mary Pritchard, shop am Blinds etc.	1-2-0
Am cheque book	2-6
Am Minute Book i'r Ysgrifennydd	1-0
Degwm ar y tir	7
Telegram i O. M. Roberts, Portmadoc	1-0
Cheque	1
Jane Jones Cefngoleu am lanhau	6-0-0
Llogau a dalwyd ar yr arian a fenthycwyd	37-6-6
Llogau i'r Bank	14-5-0
	£1886- 4-4

DERBYNIADAU AT Y CAPEL NEWYDD
RHODDION A CHASGLIADAU

	£ s c
Mr. William Jones, Penygroes	63-0-0
Capt. William Thomas, Bodlondeb	63-0-0
Capt. John Roberts, Tanybryn	49-10-10
Capt. Robert Roberts, Bryn Noddfa	45-5-0
Mrs. Ellen Ellis, Rhos	40-0-0
Capt. Robert Davies, Erw Goch	40-0-0
Mr. Wiliam Owen, Dyffryn	32-10-0
Mr. Samuel Evans, Rose Villas	30-3-0
Mr. Robert Rees, Penllel	27-1-0
Mr. Hugh Hughes, Penrhos	24-0-0
Mrs. Ellen Jones, Glanrhyd	21-16-6
Mr. James Owen, Oakfield	21-0-0
Mr. Griffith Jones, Penrhos	20-3-0
Parch. Evan Williams, Marine Terrace	20-0-6
Capt. Owen Owens, Penrhos	16-9-9
Mr. Robert Hughes, Tynlon	16-5-6
Capt. Watkin Parry, Fronolau	15-4-0
Mr. Richard Evans, Plasyngheidio	15-0-0
Capt. William Roberts, Tanybryn	15-0-0
Mr. John Thomas, Bodlondeb	15-0-0
Mr. Griffith Owen, Dyffryn	14-0-0
Mr. Evan Roberts, Pwllblew	13-10-0
Mrs. Ellen Jones, Penrhyn	13-5-0
Mr. Robert Jones, Gorphwysfa	12-2-1
Miss Mary Pritchard, Shop	10-12-6
Mrs. Catherine Owen, Fronhyfryd	10-6-0
Mr. Griffith Jones, Castle	10-5-0
Mrs. Ellen Thomas, Bwlch	10-1-0
Mr. William Jones, Mount Pleasant	8-0-6
Mrs. Mary Thomas, Fronhyfryd	7-2-0
Capt. Hugh Davies, Ty'n y coed	6-10-0
Mr. William Evans, Arddwen	6-0-2
Mr. David Jones, Jones Terrace	5-7-6
Mr. Hugh Jones, Glandwr	5-6-0
Mr. David Davies, Emporium	5-0-0
Mr. John Griffith, Penrallt	5-0-0
Mri. Thomas a R. Rowlands Tŷ Mawr	5-0-0
Mr. Robert Williams, Tai Newyddion	4-0-0
Mrs. Ann Griffiths, Bwlchglas	3-3-3
Mr. Rowland Williams, Tŷ Ucha	3-1-0
Mr. Evan Hughes, Pen'rorsedd	3-0-0
Mr. Daniel Griffith, Terfyn	3-0-0
Mr. Richard Jones, Bryncoch	3-0-0
Capt. John Jones, Schooner "Mariner"	2-12-0

Mr. Ellis Davies, Bryn'raur	2-11-0
Mrs. Jane Ellen Jones, Tŷ Coch	2-10-0
Mr. Robert Griffith, Pen'rallt	2-10-0
Mrs. Jane Jones, Crugan	2-5-0
Mr. William Jones, Hendy	2-5-0
Mr. John Hughes Pen'rorsedd	2-4-0
Mr. William Jones, Arddwen	2-3-0
Mr. William Jones, Llainfadrun	2-2-6
Mr. John Pritchard, Caergwrli	2-2-6
Mrs. Mary Thomas, Hughes Terrace	2-2-6
Mr. Henry Williams, Bryn'raur	1-15-0
Mr. Owen Owens, Caebach	1-10-4
Mr. John Williams, Iwerddon	1-10-0
Mr. John Williams, Penrhos	1-10-0
Miss Margaret Jones, Penrhos	1-10-0
Mr. W. Williams, Tŷ Newydd	1-7-6
Miss Jane Jones, Cefngolau	1-5-0
Mr. William Jones, Tŷ Isaf	1-4-6
Mr. Humphrey Hughes, Mount Pleasant	1-2-6
Mr. Ellis Humphreys, Tan'rallt	1-1-0
Mr. John Williams, Jones Terrace	1-1-0
Mrs. Catherine Jones, Bryn'raur	1-1-0
Mr. Robert Rowlands, Gors	1-1-0
Mrs. Margery Owen, Disgwylfa	1-0-9
Mrs. Ann Davies, Frondeg	1-0-3
Mr. Griffith Jones Parry, Halfway	1-0-0
Mr. Richard Parry eto	1-0-0
Mr. John Griffith, Bryn'raur Bach	1-0-0
Mrs. Ann Owen, Tu hwnt i'r ffrwd	1-0-0
Mr. John Jones, Pwllcrwn	0-15-0
Mr. Henry Parry, Lon Isaf	0-10-0
Mr. Owen Evans, Bryn'raur	0-6-0
Mr. Hugh Williams, Pen'rallt	0-5-9
Mr. Robert Evans, Cwt y gêr	0-5-1
Mrs. Sydney Evans, Llainfadrun	0-2-6
Ewyllysiwr Da	0-2-0
Casglwyd ar nos Sabothau, Tachwedd 1880, hyd Mehefin 1881	22-15-9
Mân symiau a dderbyniwyd heb fod mewn Envelopes	8-14-9
Cyfanswm y Rhoddion a'r Casgliadau	839-5-4
Derbyniwyd am yr hen Gapel	140-0-0
Derbyniwyd am Dir yr hen Gapel	100-0-0
Benthyciwyd	760-0-0
Derbyniwyd oddi wrth yr Eisteddleoedd	56-7-7
Derbyniwyd o log y Bank	2-18-6
Dyledus i'r Bank	10-13-6
	£1909-4-11

Y Parch. Evan Williams
First Minister appointed

Y Parch. Griffith Parry Hughes
Longest serving Minister

The old Methodist Chapel

CHURCH IN WALES – ST. MARY'S
(From accounts which appeared in the "North Wales Chronicle" over a hundred years ago)

Laying the Foundation Stone, 16th October, 1870

The Foundation stone of the new church in this rapidly growing neighbourhood was laid on Thursday by Mrs. Francis Lloyd Edwards of Nanhoron, who performed her part in a most graceful manner. The new building is undertaken, principally, under the auspices of the Bangor Church Extension Society, by whom a grant has been made for the erection. Proceedings commenced by singing a hymn. The 84th Psalm was read by the Rev. Ed. Pryse, Vicar of Nefyn, who afterwards read appropriate collects. The Rev. Thomas Jones, Rural Dean, addressed the gathering in English and the Revs. William Johnson and John Rowlands in Welsh. Thanks were expressed by the Vicar for all forthcoming support.

Opening of a New Church and Consecration of New Burial Ground July 18th, 1871

A most brilliant assemblage of ladies and gentlemen of Lleyn and their friends attended at Morfa Nevin on Tuesday to witness and assist in the above event. The day was beautifully fine and almost inspired us with the thought that it had been made for the occasion, especially coming, as it did, between two wet days. Lately, it has been very satisfactory to notice the increase of the Church inWales. The clergy are working zealously and the gentry and landed proprietors are helping them in a very liberal manner. The want of church accommodation has long been felt in the populous district known as Morfa Nevin, which lies midway between Nevin proper and Portinllaen. The Rev. Edward Pryse, Vicar of Nevin, in whose parish the Church is in has worked most assiduously. He is being backed by the powerful influence of R. Lloyd Edwards, Esq., Nanhoron and other of the gentry of Lleyn, and it must have been very gratifying, both to him and the worthy Squire, to see the work crowned with success on Tuesday. The church, which is remarkably well-selected, is approached by a pretty green lane from the turnpike road and presents a very neat appearance. The land, to the extent of three-quarters of an acre was given by R. Lloyd Edwards, Esq. The architect was Mr. W. Pritchard of Nanhoron, and the contractor, Mr. Robert Jones, Caernarvon. The church is built of stone which was generously given by Mr. Farren of Llanaelhaearn. It is lined inside with brick, which will prevent damp appearing. The cost of much of the work of building and the furniture of the church together with the levelling of the burial ground, the erection of the boundary wall and the greater part of the cartage of material has been paid for by R. Lloyd Edwards, Esq. The timbers of the roof were supplied by the Eryri Steam Mills, Caernarvon and the Font erected by Mr. Hugh Jones of Caernarvon.

The little church was crowded to excess for all the opening services. At 11.a.m. the Lord Bishop delivered an earnest discourse and afterwards a large number of clergy in their surplices accompanied the former for the ceremony of Consecrating the Burial Ground. At the conclusion, the following ladies collected:- Mrs. Owen Evans, Broom Hall, attended by R. Lloyd Edwards, Esq., Nanhoron; Mrs. Thomas Jones, Llanengan, attended by Owen Evans, Esq., Broom Hall; and Mrs. Francis Edwards, Nanhoron attended by T. Ellis, Esq.

At 3 p.m. the Litany was read and afterwards a most eloquent sermon was preached by the Rev. E. Edwards, Llanfechell. In the evening the Rev. G. Griffiths, Rector of Machynlleth, preached from Deut. XXXV, v 17. The Welsh services were extremely well attended, all standing room being occupied. There must have been between six and seven hundred present during the whole day's services and all these showed an unmistakable interest in the proceedings. A most "recherché" luncheon was provided by Mrs. Pryse, the Vicarage, at Rhiwlas. Need we add that the visitors were most thankful for it and did justice to the good things so liberally supplied.

The collection for the day amounted to £33 17s 10d.

St. Mary's Church – always known locally as Eglwys Bach (The Small Church)

Development in Transport

The first roadway through Morfa Nefyn had been built in the first decade of the 19th century following the establishment of the Porthdinllaen Turnpike Trust by an Act of Parliament in 1803. The Trust with successive renewals of its powers lasted until 1874 but it was never a profitable enterprise and failed to fulfil its obligations. The year 1862 resulted in a number of complaints against the organisation when it was alleged that its roads were throughout deeply rutted, muddy and otherwise uneven because of the indiscriminate dumping of large stones. In 1864 it was reported that the road between the Boduan Toll-gate and Bryn Cynan, was in an atrocious condition and that years had elapsed since the last attempt at its repair had been made. In 1869 it had an income of £747 but a debt of £1,325 and it never developed as its original promoters had envisaged. The Porthdinllaen Turnpike Trust yielded its powers in 1874 which meant that the responsibility for maintaining the roads fell on local parishes. In 1898 the County Council became the relevant highway authority and this did result in some improvements which were accelerated with the developments in motorised transport.

The roads in 1850 were quite inadequate and during bad weather were virtually unusable. Movements of goods and people along these roads in the 1850s would have been mainly by horse and cart and donkeys. It was a common site to see donkeys in twos and threes drawing carts, or just saddled up with eggs, butter etc. or with goods from the ships that came in to Porthdinllaen. A gentleman called Richard Williams who lived in a thatched cottage with a stable near the present Parc Stores ran a cart with donkeys between Pwllheli and Morfa. Most small farmers in the area also supplemented their income by acting as carriers.

Goods and people in the latter half of the century were transported by some form of horse drawn vehicle – ranging from a small pony and trap to large four in hand coaches which could convey up to 16 or 17 passengers. The coaches and their drivers became very important in the life of the village and particularly after 1867 when the railway reached Pwllheli.

One of the early coach owners and drivers which served Morfa Nefyn was Richard Davies a young man from Pwllheli who had married and settled in Edern. He ran a coaching business from Edern via Pwllheli to Caernarfon. He ran his coach in relays and kept 4 horses at Edern, Pwllheli and Clynnog. He left Edern each day at 6 a.m. and arrived at Caernarfon by 10, in time to catch the train. The coach returned at 4 p.m. and reached Edern about 8 at night. After 8 years in Edern he took over the Nanhoron Arms, (Tŷ Cerrig, Three Herrings) Nefyn and from then onwards he ran his coach between Nefyn and Pwllheli. When Richard Davies retired he went to live in Plasyngheidio where he died in 1917 aged 79 years. He was always referred to locally as "Dic y Goits". Another coach company was based at Penpalment Nefyn and John Elias followed by his son William Jones ran coaches from Edern to Pwllheli via Nefyn. John Elias' grandson Evan Jones lived at Jones Terrace for many years and was a bus driver with Crosville until his retirement.

Griffith Jones, one time driver for Richard Davies, started up on his own account and ran a four in hand and three in hand from Edern to Pwllheli. He kept the Castle Inn, Morfa Nefyn which was built in 1866 and he kept his horses in stables attached to the inn. The coach ran 6 days a week, Sundays excepted and the horses were rested and fed at the Farmer's Arms, Efailnewydd.

William Jones, Cae'r Pwll drove a four in hand about 1885. The coach started at 8 a.m. at Edern, reaching Pwllheli at 10, returning about 5 to arrive back in Edern at 7 p.m. William Hughes,

Jones Terrace drove the coach for 15 years before he opened his greengrocer's shop in the village.

Around the same time yet another coach was operated from Tir Gwenith. It was referred to locally as the Coach Fawr and carried 28 people – 11 inside and 17 outside. It ran a regular service from Llangwnadl via Tudweiliog, Edern, Morfa, Nefyn to Pwllheli.

Coaching continued to be popular until travel by horses gradually gave way to the motor vehicle in the years leading up to the first World War.

In 1906 the Cambrian Railways introduced a motor bus service from Pwllheli railway station to Nefyn, Morfa and Edern with two vehicles. They had been manufactured by the Orion Company and registered as CC 162 and CC 163. They continued to be the only service until 1912 when Tir Gwenith purchased a motor bus from the firm Karrier in Huddersfield and ran a service to Pwllheli on Monday, Wednesday, Friday and Saturday. The bus left Morfa (outside present chip shop) at 9.05 a.m. arriving in Pwllheli at 9.30 a.m. and returning at 5.15 p.m. The single fare was 1 shilling and the return 1/6d

In the following year a group of people from Nefyn formed the Nefyn and District Motor Omnibus Company Limited managed and supervised by Owen Henry Parry, Nanhoron Arms. The following year the two local companies joined forces and competed with the Cambrian later G.W.R. until 1925 when the latter bought them out. One of the drivers on these early Nefyn buses was a gentleman called Thomas Jones who resided at Y Fron, Nefyn. Unfortunately Thomas was killed while bringing home a bus load of children from Pwllheli School one Friday afternoon in 1916. As the bus reached the crest of Boduan Hill, the engine stalled, the brakes failed to hold it and it accelerated backwards down the steep slope. He desperately tried to stop it by reversing into a gateway on the side of the road but the bus overturned with fatal results. The driver died and several of the young passengers were injured, some quite seriously.

Soon after the First World War another bus company was established in Nefyn known as the Blue Bus Company. It was the brainchild of a local hairdresser Mr. Gawen Hughes who by creating this company introduced fierce competition into the transport business. One of the first drivers for the company was a relative of Mr. Hughes from Liverpool called Ritchie Harris. Another popular driver for the company was always referred to as Johnnie Blue – very few people were familiar with his surname.

In 1930 the G.W.R. amalgamated their bus company with a firm from Wrexham to form Western Transport who in turn were taken over by Crosville in 1933. The Blue Bus Company continued in opposition for a time but later in the 30s it was also taken over by Crosville who until the 1990s had a monopoly on public transport from Morfa to Pwllheli. Prior to and during the Second World War they also ran a direct service to Caernarfon over the Rivals. By this decade the wheel seems to have gone full circle and again a local Nefyn company is responsible for the journey to town and back.

The railway came to Pwllheli in 1867 but did not advance any further into the Llŷn Peninsula. There were, however, numerous schemes and plans submitted, surveys made and considerable efforts to raise money for the extension of the railway to Porthdinllaen. Plans had been submitted in 1845 by the G.W.R. for a railway from Worcester beyond Pwllheli to Porthdinllaen. A year previously a gentleman by the name of Henry Archer with the backing of London based promoters formed the North Wales Railway Company. Their plan was to build a railway from Caernarfon to Porthdinllaen with a tunnel through the Rivals and a viaduct across Nant Gwrtheyrn. Financial problems and clash of personalities eventually led to the company being disbanded and no railway.

In 1877 the Cambrian Railway had authority to continue the railway to Porthdinllaen but no steps were taken to construct the line – mainly for economic and financial reasons.

In 1884 an Act was passed which authorised the construction of a railway from Pwllheli to Porthdinllaen by a company of mainly local proprietors including Love Jones Parry of Madryn. The line was to terminate near the Lifeboat House but the Harbour Company insisted on it ending near Whitehall. As the Harbour company was in the hands of the Madryn family, negotiations were probably amicable enough.

The Company was authorised to raise capital of £120,000 in £10 shares but apart from getting the time limit extended in 1888 and again in 1892 the Company did nothing because the necessary capital was not subscribed. After the expiration of its powers in 1897 the Porthdinllaen Railway Company called it a day.

Ever hopeful another group of local people promoted the Pwllheli, Nevin and Porthdinllaen Light Railway and deposited their plans in 1900. A prospectus advertising the sale of land in Morfa Nefyn in 1908 included the following statement.

> *"It is probable that when the proposed scheme for the new railway from Pwllheli to this district is carried through then the station will be placed at a convenient spot to this property".*

This was the field which existed between the main road and the church.

Again investment did not materialise and competition of a new kind was now in the offing. The rapid development of road transport was the nail in the coffin of Porthdinllaen's hopes of ever being connected by rail to the main line system, yet the rumours abounded and in 1913 the Cambrian obtained powers to extend its line from Pwllheli to Porthdinllaen. The War in 1914 put an end to the scheme and this time it really was the end.

First buses to Pwllheli

Mr. John Hughes – known locally as "Johnny Blue" from the days when he was a driver for the Blue Buses based at Nefyn. He was a driver with Crosville for many years before his retirement.

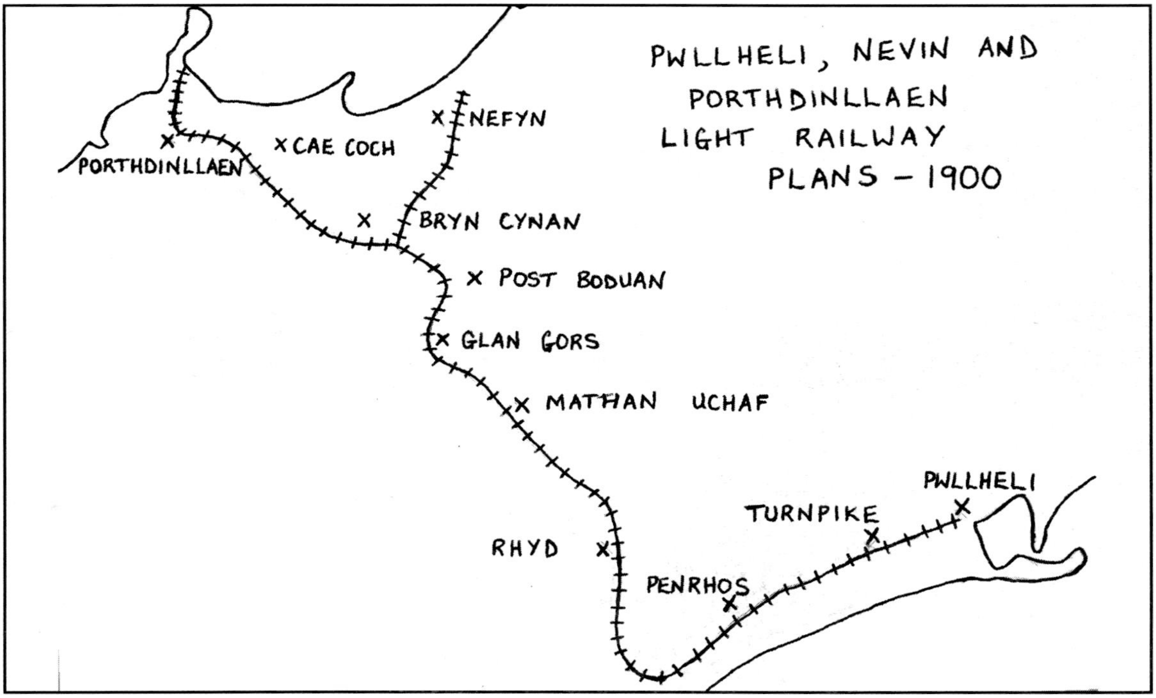

A coach setting off from Pwllheli to Morfa and beyond.

The last small coaster to deliver coal and other goods to Morfa Nefyn.

Tourism

The development of tourism during the last 100 years is an important chapter in the history of Morfa Nefyn. The popularity of the area is due entirely to the fact that it more than lives up to its designation as an area of outstanding natural beauty. The prominent rocky headland of Porthdinllaen sheltering a wide bay with the Rivals and the mountains of Snowdonia beyond forms a background to the most impressive vista on the North Wales Coast.

Travellers have been coming to this area for centuries but in the main they were men with an interest in botany, geology and history. The masses were not attracted as communication particularly by road was very poor. It was the construction of the railway to Pwllheli, the improvement in motorised transport and better roads that led to the beginning of tourism in this area prior to the First World War. Compulsory annual holidays for workers during the 20th century, accelerated the development.

The list that follows is from a guide book of 1912 and names some of the guest houses in the village at that time.

Mrs. A. Davies, Islwyn, detached; 2 sitting-rooms, 6 bedrooms, bathroom (h. and c), furnished or attendance.
Mrs. G. Owen, Erw Goch, detached; 3 sitting-rooms, 8 bedrooms, bathroom (h. and c.), furnished or attendance.
Mrs. L. Hart, Plas Tirion, detached; 2 sitting-rooms, 7 bedrooms, bathroom (h. and c), furnished or attendance.
Mrs. E. Davies, Bronwylfa, detached; 2 sitting-rooms, 6 bedrooms, with or without attendance.
Mrs. Roberts, Brynnoddfa, detached; 3 sitting-rooms, 8 bedrooms; apartments.
Mrs. E. R. Hughes, Rhiwlas, detached; 3 sitting-rooms, 7 bedrooms, furnished or attendance.
Mrs. D. Jones, Terfyn, detached; 2 sitting-rooms, 6 bedrooms, furnished or attendance.
Mrs. K. Jones, Rhos, detached; 3 sitting-rooms, 4 bedrooms, with or without attendance.
Mrs. Hughes, Newlands, detached; 3 sitting-rooms, 6 bedrooms, with or without board.
Mrs. Pritshow, Monarfon, semi-detached; 2 sitting-rooms, 7 bedrooms, furnished or apartments, garage.
Mrs. C. Davies, Moneifion, semi-detached; 2 sitting-rooms, 7 bedrooms, attendance, bath (h. and c.)
Mrs. J. Hughes, Glan Eirian, semi-detached; 2 sitting-rooms, 5 bedrooms, with or without attendance.
Mrs. R. Jones, Glan Arfor, semi-detached; 2 sitting-rooms, 5 bedrooms, furnished.
Mrs. J. Jones, Fair View, semi-detached; 2 sitting-rooms, 3 bedrooms, apartments.
Mrs. E. Owens, Belle Vue, semi-detached; 2 sitting-rooms, 3 bedrooms, furnished or apartments.
Mrs. H. Roberts, Moranedd, semi-detached; 2 sitting-rooms, 5 bedrooms, with or without attendance.

Mrs. A. Jones, Talarfor, semi-detached; 2 sitting-rooms, 5 bedrooms, apartments
Mrs. Jones, Glanrafon House, semi-detached; 2 sitting-rooms, 5 bedrooms, with or without board.
Mrs. M. Williams, Llys Alaw, semi-detached; 2 sitting-rooms, 5 bedrooms, apartments.
Mrs. J. Herbert, Ael-y-bryn, semi-detached; 2 sitting-rooms, 3 bedrooms, apartments.
Mrs. J. Williams, Glanogwen, semi-detached; 2 sitting-rooms, 2 bedrooms, apartments.
Mrs. M. E. Williams, Meifod, semi-detached; 3 sitting-rooms, 3 bedrooms, apartments.
Mrs. E. Williams, Heulfre, detached; 2 sitting-rooms, 5 bedrooms, furnished, bath (h. and c.)
Mrs. C. Davies, Penrhos, semi-detached; 2 sitting-rooms, 3 bedrooms, furnished.
Mrs. G. Williams, Bwlch cottage, detached; 2 sitting-rooms, 3 bedrooms, furnished.
Mrs. M. Owen, Marina, semi-detached; 2 sitting-rooms, 4 bedrooms, furnished; on beach.
Miss J. Thomas, Môr Awelon, detached; 1 sitting-room, 2 bedrooms, attendance; on beach.

The next list shows the tourists who stayed in Morfa during the first week of August 1912. The number of visitors is surprising and it is interesting to note where they came from.

Hollies – Mrs. Whitfield
Mr. and Mrs. Verso, Liverpool
Master A. Verso
Master F. Verso
Miss Crossley
Mr. D. Wilson

Glanmorfa – Mrs. Williams
Mr. and Mrs. Cartwright and family, Birmingham
Mr. and Mrs. Bodley

Glanaber – Mrs. Morgan Owen
Mrs. Gregory, Southport
Misses Gregory
Mr. and Mrs. Hamnett and 2 children, Stockport

Glan'rafon house – Mrs. Jones
Mrs. Drover and family, Birkenhead
Miss Hurley

Glan Ogwen – Mrs. Williams
Mr. & Mrs. Vincent & 2 daughters, Leicester

Rocket View – Mrs. Jones
Mr. and Mrs. Evans, London
Miss Broomhead, Cheshire
Miss Jones

Sea View – Mrs. Thomas
Dr. and Mrs. Miller and family, Preston

Meifod – Mrs. Evans
Mr. and Mrs. Plant, Chester
Miss Parkeman, Derby
Miss Houston
Dr. D. G. Collins and son, Brosley

Newlands – Mrs. Hughes
Mr. and Mrs. Philpott, Birmingham
Miss McEnnan, Liverpool
Mr. and Mrs. Bradbury and child, Hale
Misses Buckley
Mr. and Mrs. Strury and family, Rugby

Mon Eifion
Mr. and Mrs. Phillips and son, Sutton Coalfield
Dr and Mrs. Holmes and family, Liverpool

Mon Arfon
Sir David and Lady Gamble, nurses and children, Liverpool
Mrs. R. Roberts, Bootle

Moranedd – Mrs. Roberts
Rev. & Mrs. Masher & son, Heaton Norris
Miss Clayton
Mr. Beckett, Manchester
Misses Irving
Mr Cope

Talarfor
Mr. And Mrs. Hoare, 2 children and nurse, Rugby
Mr. and Mrs. Stocks, 4 children & nurse

Hen Blas –
Mr. and Mrs. Webster

Glasfryn –
Mrs. Guppy, Slough
Mr. and Mrs. Gooderson

Sunnyside – Mrs. Hughes
Mr. And Mrs Macirone O'Brien and family, Dublin
Miss Macirone
Miss S Macirone, France
Miss Evans, Burton-onTrent
Misses Brown

Aelybryn – Mrs. Herbert
Mr. and Mrs. F. W. Edgecombe, Blundellsands
Miss Hall
Miss T. S. Hall

No. 1 Crugan –
Mr. and Mrs. Wayatt and family, London

No. 2 Crugan –
Mr. and Mrs. Taylor, Rickmansworth
Miss B. Taylor
Miss M. Taylor
Miss Salmon, London
Miss Potts
Miss Bott, Birmingham

Ivy House – Mrs. Davies
Mrs. Gibbins, London
Miss Gibbins

Llwyn Onn – Mr. & Mrs. Harrison & family, Birmingham

Glan Menai – Mrs. Griffiths
Mr. and Mrs. W. T. Stanton, Handsworth
Misses Doris and Olive Stanton

Rhianfa – Mrs. Jones
Mr. A. W. P. Langstone, Withington
Mr. M. Goodier
Mr. E. Goodier
Mr. H. W. Bidmead
Miss Bates, Cheltenham
Miss Marston
Miss Houston

Glan Noddfa –
Mr. Owen, Oakfield

Rivals View –
Mr and Mrs Sherwood and family, Sutton Coalfield
Miss Cape

Trigfan – Miss Lloyd Williams
Mr & Mrs Prime, West Bridgfort
Miss Preston, Notts

Belle Vue – Mrs. Owens
Mr. Henry H. Elkes & family, Wallasey

Voelas – Miss Jones
Miss E. M. Pritchard, Wrexham
Miss F. Pritchard
Misses Pritchard

Llys Heli – Mrs. Liversidge
Mr. Joen Francis, Nythfa, Wrexham
The Misses Francis

This pattern of private house accommodation was a means of supplementing the family income and the money would also help to defray the cost of running the large houses which many of them were. In the interwar years more and more houses in the village would start taking in paying guests and even the smallest cottages such as those in Penrhos could ingeniously manage by erecting huts in the back garden where the family would live from May to September.

During this period the same families used to arrive year after year and more often than not stayed in the same houses and developed friendly relationships with the local people. Richards, Murray, Cooper, Buckley and of course Waldi are some names that come to mind and each of them still maintain a close connection with Morfa Nefyn either as residents or second home owners. I believe the Waldi family have been coming to Morfa for well over 100 years.

The attraction of the village has always focused around the beach and the golf club and the regulars who came year after year seem to have had this dual interest. The beach at that time and before the local authority built the stone revetment was extremely popular particularly the stretch of lovely yellow sand there used to be between Bwlch and Cerrig Gleision. Along here there used to be a long row of wooden beach huts every summer which people hired and used throughout their holiday. With the little wooden shop selling sweets, hiring deck chairs etc., no jet skis or fast speedboats, it was a much more civilised scene than it is today but I do admit to being somewhat prejudiced.

During the interwar years two hotels were established in the village – the Cecil and the Linksway and they were both very popular, successful small hotels.

Thanks to shorter working hours and increased spending power, ordinary people had more time and money to spend on holidays. Morfa Nefyn like every other seaside village benefited from this and more and more people came here to enjoy their summer holidays.

Following the Second World War and particularly during the last quarter of the 20th Century, tourism has undergone immense changes. Many social factors have led to a marked decline in the traditional British guest house family holiday and one can now count on the fingers of one hand the number of houses in Morfa Nefyn who cater for tourists. This is very different to 1912 and even in the peak month of August one sees very few tourists staying in the village itself. There has, however, been a surge in demand for other types of holiday with the tourists in the main staying in their own holiday homes, in caravans and campsites or coming to the village in groups for short midweek or weekend breaks for golfing, fishing or any other activity which might interest them.

The tourist industry brings considerable economic benefit to the area but it does create problems. It is also very difficult to control the varied interests of the modern day tourist. Peace and quietness with a pleasant swim does often clash with noisy jet skis and high powered boats and on occasions the 4 x 4 seems to take over the beach to the annoyance of many families with young children. The seasonal influx of people can impose excessive demands on public utilities and services and cause traffic congestion and even spoil a lovely beach. The social consequences of second homes must be addressed and any friction avoided where possible and I am sure that many local people like myself will keep a careful watch on the stewardship of the National Trust over what we consider to be our beach.

The Golf Course – has been a major tourist attraction for almost 100 years
This photograph shows the old Club House which was destroyed by fire in the 1920s

September 5th 1902 Coxswain – John Jermy Jones
Tourists have visited the lifeboat station for over 100 years

Tourists on the beach – Prior to First World War

Above – the beach in the 1930s – note the bathing huts

Dressed for the beach 1930s style

I have included the verses that follow in the belief that they might be of interest to local Welsh people particularly those in my age group who may well remember some of the people mentioned.

The gentleman writing under the pseudonym Glan Cefni was I believe a soldier who spent some time at Aber Geirch during the 1st World War.

Many will remember with affection Elen Jones (Nell Hen Blas) who lived on the beach for many years.

DAETH AWR Y FFARWEL DDU

Mae'r awen dan ei briwiau,
Daeth awr y ffarwel ddu;
Ac anodd iawn yw cefnu
Ar hen gyfeillion cu;
Aeth blwyddyn gyfan heibio
Fel undydd unnos bron;
Ac heddyw rhaid ffarwelio
Y fro addunol hon.

Ar ddechre'n nghan dywedaf
Mai camp i unrhyw ddyn
Yw canfod gwell dyngarwyr
Na charedigion Lleyn;
Tra bum yn gwylio'r glannau
Fe dreuliais lawer awr
Ar aelwyd hwn ac arall
Mae 'mharch i'r oll yn fawr.

Yn awr rhaid canu ffarwel
i lethrau Aber Geirch,
lle bum yn gwrando'n ddifyr
Ar wehyriadau'r meirch.
Ffawel i lôn y gwartheg
A llwybr pen y clawdd.
Ei gerdded pan yn dywyll
Nid oedd yn orchwyl hawdd.

Ffarwel i drwyn y Penrhyn,
Y môr a'i donnau croch
Ffarwel i Ogo'r Bwgan
A theulu cu Tŷ Coch.
Ffarwel i "Warff" y "Dora"
Yr Hen Blas a'r White Hall;
Fe ddof i'ch gweled eilwaith
Os byth caf ddod yn ôl.
Ffarwel i'r Bwlch a Gwynfor
A Bardd Disgwylfa Bach;
i'r Foelas a Bod Awen,
Rhaid i mi ganu'n iach.
Ffarwel i Tomi Bodfan
a Lizzie, Ty'n-y-Mur,
Ffarwel i Wil Môr Annedd,
Mae'i galon fel y dur.

Ffarwel i Capten Williams
Shop John a Meic Cae Coch
Y modur sydd yn dyfod
Mi glywaf sŵn ei gloch.
Ffarwel i'r Bardd "Myfyrian"
A William Hughes y "Goets"
Rhaid galw yn Shop Percy
i brynu watch a "brooch".

Ffarwel i'r cyfaill Watcyn,
Y postman chwim ei droed
Ffarwel i Kate, Hope Villa,
Bryn'r Aur a Maelfa Lloyd;
Ffarwel i Shop y Rhandir,
Bryn Noddfa ac Ashdene;
Ffarwel i'r coed fu'n gysgod,
i mi rhag gwres yr hin.

Ffarwel i Mair Angorfa,
Ac Ifan Thomas wiw,
Ffarwel i Huw, Bryn Heulog
a Henry hoff Rock View;
Ffarwel i Ben-yr-Orsedd;
Tŷ Mawr a Tacho Wyn;
Fy llygad sydd yn Llŷn.

Ffarwel i Garn Bodfean
A'r Llan sydd yn y coed;
Wrth rodio rhwng y beddau
Dywedodd William Lloyd –
"Mae gobaith gŵr o'r rhyfel,
Does gobaith neb o'r bedd,"
Ddychwelais innau unwaith
O'r gad yn llon fy ngwedd.

Morfa Nefyn
Glan Cefni

FFARWEL

Ffarwel i bentre Edeyrn
A chamfa yr Allt Goch
Wrth gofio am fy ffrindiau
Daw deigryn tros fy moch.
Ffarwel i'r llwybrau gerddais
I lawr at Borthtinllaen,
Ffarwel i goed y Terfyn,
Rhaid i mi frisio'n mlaen.

Ffarwel i Gefn y Morfa
Ffarwel i Lôn Pen Rhos.
Wrth gerdded hon y canais
Fy nghan i Morfydd dlos;
Ffarwel i bonc y rhiwlas
Ffarwel i'r Castle Inn
Lle ca i sychedig ddiod
Pan fydd y dwr yn brin.

Ffarwel i Nellie, Isfryn
A Lizzie Pant y Lôn,
Ffarwel i O. M. Williams
Y cerddor pêr ei dôn.
Ffarwel i'r Heddwas Evans
Ac Owen bach y Bryn.
Ffarwel i'r llwyni eithin
Sydd ger y Bwthyn Gwyn.

Ffarwel i swyddfa'r gwifrau
A'r sawyr brwnt ei flas.
Ffarwel i Lôn Bodlondeb
A'i throeon ceimion câs.
Ffarwel i goed y Vicerage
Bryn Beuno a Pen Rallt.
Ffarwel i'r eneth siriol
Rodd raffau am fy ngwallt.

Ffarwel i Ysgol Nefyn
Yr Eglwys a'r hotel.
Ffarwel i Dwr y Gwylwyr
Y Groes a'i genod del.
Ffarwel i goed Fron Oleu
A llidiart Tacho Ddu
Ffarwel i Roli'r Dyffryn
Fy nghyfaill mwyaf cu.

Ffarwel i Fferm Bryn Cynnan
Lle bum i'n cario gwair.
A llawer noswaith wedyn
Wrth ddod yn ôl o'r ffair.
Ffarwel i John a William
Y gwas ac Alun bach.
Cewch gennyf air o'm hanes
Os byddaf byw ac iach.

Glan Cefni

HEN GYFEILLION

Chwith yw colli hen gyfeillion
A chymdogion o'r iawn ryw.
Rhoddai'r teulu aur y ddaear
Am eu cael yn ôl yn fyw.

Pentre'r Morfa ddeil i wylo
Am gyfeillion amser maith
Ond maent hwy yn berffaith hapus
Wedi cyrraedd pen y daith.

Trist yw myned trwy y Groeslon
Wal Cae Coch sydd heddiw'n fud,
Mae yr hen gyfeillion annwyl
Wedi mynd i arall fyd.

Cadair wag sydd ar yr aelwyd.
Gwag ei sedd yn Eglwys Dduw.
Ond mae'r cyfan gyda'i gilydd
Yn y wlad lle nad oes briw.

Anodd ydyw peidio wylo
Pan mae'r galon fach yn drist.
Wylodd Mair a wylodd Martha
Ac fe wylodd Iesu Grist.

Ceisiwn ninnau, rai sy'n aros
Roi ein baich ar fraich yr Iôr.
Digyfnewid ydyw'r Iesu,
Mae ei gariad fel y môr.

Elen Jones
Hen Blas, Morfa Nefyn

A sketch of Pen Cim – Circa 1885

Pen Cim – 1890s

Pen Cim – 1893

Brick works jetty and lime kiln

A typical sea captain's house – the motif above the centre window is a clue to its location.

Porthdinllaen Farm – for many years the biggest employer in the district

Jones Terrace – the three children (from left to right) were Hughie Evans (Tŷ Capel), Miss Davies (Bron Wylfa) and John Pierce Hughes. All three youngsters spent most of their lives in the district.

John Pierce Hughes (left) was for many years a groundsman at the Golf Club and later took over his father's green grocery business. He poses in the photograph with trophies won for gardening at which he excelled.

Note the entrance to the Castle Inn and the regulars waiting for opening time

The child with cycle was Eric Jones who worked in his father's garage for many years

This hostelry is on the outskirts of the village and now a thriving establishment

The Castle Inn – Popular in the early years of the last century

Have you had a meal here recently

This crossroad will never look the same

A busy day in the 1920s

A very busy day – a few years later

A group outside the Baptist Chapel – early last century

Children and young people near the Methodist Chapel

A group of local young people enjoy a picnic on the beach

Members of a group who used the small house as a reading room – Circa 1910

A local drama group – outside the old Village Hall

A local Youth Club in the 1950s

W.I. members outside their centre in Church Lane
All the women were Welsh and from the village

Merched y Wawr

English people refer to Abergeirch as Cable Bay.

The telegraph cables to Ireland were connected to the building on the right

The small cottage on the left was home to Jane Jones who lived there alone following the death of her parents and elder sister. She was quite a character and known locally as Sian Abergeirch.

J. Glynne Davies in one of his poems describes the scene then and now.

Ond tawel iawn oedd bwthyn Siân
cyn mynd yn fyrddyn;
Hen Siân a'i hieir, cath, barcud, bran,
holl deulu'r llecyn

Mae'r cwbl wedi mynd ers tro
pwy sy'n eu cofio?
Sŵn tonnau'n torri ar y gro
fydd yno heno.

Rear of Penygroes – W. P. Roberts repaired bicycles there before opening his garage on Lôn Penrhos

Lloyd's Stores – delivery van at the side

Part 2

Mariners at War

Casualties of War

The Commonwealth War Graves Commission was established by Royal Charter in 1917. Its duties are to mark and maintain the graves of men and women of the Commonwealth who were killed in the two World Wars of the last century and to build memorials to those who have no known grave. One such memorial is that at Tower Hill in London which commemorates the men from the Merchant Navy and Fishing Fleets who gave their lives for their country and have no grave but the sea.

THE TOWER HILL MEMORIAL
(Note the Tower of London in the background)

The 12,000 men who died during World War 1 are listed in the covered, vaulted corridor which was designed by Edwin Lutyens and unveiled by Queen Mary on 12th December 1928. This is linked to the 1939-45 memorial (designed by Edward Maufe) by a flight of stone steps, leading into a sunken garden. The names of the 24,000 seamen are on the bronze panels set against the retaining walls of the garden. At set intervals around the wall are seven figures, each one representing one of the seas of the world. In the centre of the garden is a small pool engraved as a compass.

Between the memorials are two tall columns against which stand sculptured figures representing an Officer and a Seaman of the Merchant Service. All names are arranged in alphabetical order under the name of the ship they were lost on.

The reason I am writing about this imposing memorial is because the names of 12 men from Morfa Nefyn are engraved on it. In the following pages I have attempted to document the tragic manner in which each of these men lost their lives and in doing so my intention is to perpetuate their memory and in a small way pay tribute to the fact that they paid the ultimate price. I also consider it important to let younger people know about what has happened in the fairly recent past.

I have written in length about a few of the men because the information was available and it is no disrespect to those whom I could find very little about. Each account is headed by extracts from the certification records of the War Graves Commission. The lack of information and incorrect spelling in some cases are as they appear in the originals.

Close up of the Sunken Garden – names are inscribed on the panels fixed to the surrounding wall

In Memory of
Master GRIFFITH OWEN

H.M.T. "North Wales", Mercantile Marine
who died age 45
on 24 October 1916

Son of the late Capt. Henry and Catherine Owen of Morfa Nevin, Canravonshire; husband of Jane Owen, of "Erw Goch", Morfa Nevin. In November, 1914, while in command of another H.M.T. "North Wales" his ship was caught and sunk off Coronel, South America, by German cruiser "Dresden". He was made prisoner and released after battle of Falkland Islans.
Remembered with honour.

In Memory of
Carpenter WILLIAM WILLIAMS

S.S. "North Wales" (London) Mercantile Marine
who died age 26
on 24 October 1916

Son of William Williams, of Glan Morfa, Morfa Nevin, Carnarvonshire, and the late Mary Williams.
Remembered with honour.

Captain Griffith Owen of Erw Goch was master of the vessel North Wales and a member of the crew was 26 year old ship's carpenter William Williams. The latter's home was Glan Morfa, one of the terraced houses situated across the road from the Captain's home in Lôn Isaf. Williams' mother had died in 1915 but he was survived by his father Captain William Williams and his sister Ellen. Capt. Owen left a wife, Mrs. Jane Owen and three boys.

The ship North Wales was on a voyage from Hull to America when disaster struck. She sank off the Isles of Scilly in October 1916, presumably torpedoed by a submarine with the loss of all 30 members of the crew. Some unidentified bodies were washed ashore and were buried in the parish church of Sennen Cove, Cornwall, where a headstone records the disaster. It was the second occasion for this to happen to Capt. Owen. His previous ship (also named North Wales) had been sunk in the Pacific Ocean off the coast of Chile in South America on 16th November 1914. This ship was sunk by the German light cruiser "Dresden". The crew were taken prisoner but were released before the cruiser itself was sunk following the naval battle off the Falkland Islands.

Both vessels belonged to the North Shipping Co. of Tyneside, a company which had been founded by Hugh Roberts, a native of Edern. He was the son of Llain Hir and at an early age he went to sea becoming Master in his early 20's. He became friendly with and eventually formed a partnership with a slate merchant from Newcastle called Edward Beck.

In Memory of
Boatswain WILLIAM THOMAS

S.S. "Canganian" (Cardiff), Mercantile Marine
who died age 50
on 17 November, 1916

Son of the late Hugh and Ellen Thomas; husband of Jane Thomas (nee Jones), of Sea View, Morfa Nevin, Carnarvonshire.
Born at Henborth, Edeyon.
Remembered with honour

In Memory of
Carpenter HUGH THOMAS

S.S. "Canganian" (Cardiff), Mercantile Marine
who died age 19
on 17 November, 1916

Son of Jane Thomas, of Sea View, Morfa Nevin, Carnarvonshire, and the late William Thomas
Remembered with honour

In Memory of
Seaman HUGH DAVID OWEN

S.S. "Canganian" (Cardiff), Mercantile Marine
who died age 23
on 17 November, 1916

Son of Griffith and Margaret Owen, of Isfryn, Morfa Nevin, Carnarvonshire
Remembered with honour

17th November 1916 was a very sad day for Morfa Nefyn when the S.S. Canganian was struck by a mine off Montrose. She had sailed from Methil with a cargo of coal for Scapa Flow whilst on service as an Admiralty Collier. Hearsay has it that there was only one survivor namely John Jones (Sion 'R'iard) of Porthdinllaen It was a tragedy for Mr. and Mrs. Owen to lose their son Hugh but a double tragedy for Mrs. Jane Thomas, Sea View, on losing both her husband and son on the same day.

The vessel Canganian belonged to the Golden Cross Line of Cardiff. This company had been established by two brothers from Pwllparc in Edern and the Company was always referred to locally as Llongau Pwll Parc. It was customary for the ships to be manned by sailors from the Llŷn Peninsula.

In Memory of
Master J OWEN

"Beacon Light", Mercantile Marine
who died
on 19 February, 1918.

Remembered with honour

In Memory of
Carpenter WILLIAM JAMES OWEN

S.S. "Beacon Light" (Liverpool), Mercantile Marine
who died age 40
on 19 February, 1918

Son of the late James and Jan Owen; husband of Grace Alice Owen (nee Roberts), of Bodfewing, Upper Llandurog, Carnarvonshire.
Born at Nevin.

Remembered with honour

The above were two brothers and the sons of James Owen and his wife who lived at Oakfield, Lôn Uchaf. The father had been a well known ship builder at Porthdinllaen but with the demise in shipbuilding he diversified and became a successful flour dealer. The youngest son John became a very well known Methodist minister.

In Memory of
Fireman JAMES JONES

S.S. "Broomhill" (Newcastle), Mercantile Marine
who died age 43
on 10 May, 1917
Son of Robert and Ellen Jones; husband of Ellen Jones (nee Davies), of Bodfan, Morfa Nevin, Carnarvonshire.
Born at Nevin.
Remembered with honour

James, 44, was a native of Nefyn who came to live in Bodfan, Lôn Penrhos, when he married Ellen. His parents were Robert and Ellen Jones who sadly lost their other son Robert, 37, on the same ship.

In Memory of
Second Officer ELIZEUS GRIFFITH JONES

S.S. Ulea (Glasgow), Merchant Navy
who died age 65
on 28 October, 1941
Husband of M.G. Jones, of Morfa Nevin, Caernarvonshire.
Master Mariner, Merchant Navy.
Remembered with honour

Elizeus Griffith Jones was Second Officer on the 1,574 ton steam freighter Ulea of Glasgow when she was torpedoed on a voyage from Huelva in Spain to Oban with a cargo of copper pyrites. 19 members of a crew of 28 lost their lives as a result of the attack in position 41° 17.N, 21.40W.

The attacker was U-boat 432 under the command of Heinz-Otto Schultz who was one of Germany's top U-boat aces responsible for sinking 19 ships. Schultz, himself died when his U-boat was sunk with all hands on 23rd November 1944 as a result of depth charges from an American B-24 Liberator aircraft.

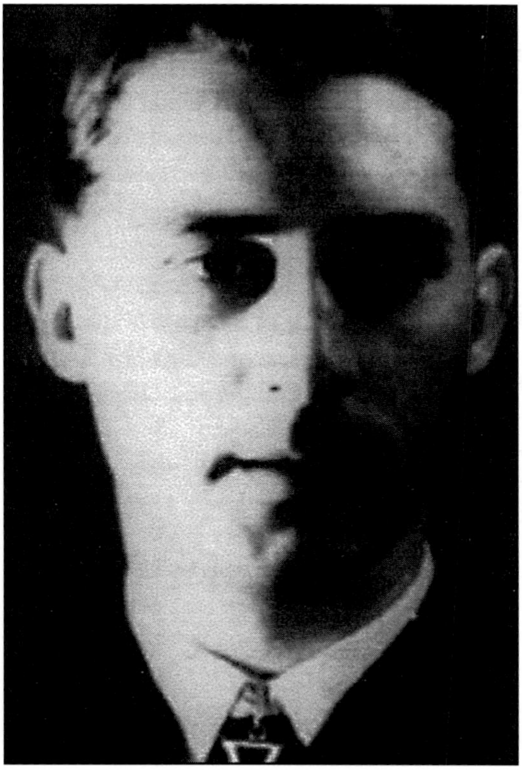

Heinz-Otto Schultz

In Memory of
Carpenter EDWIN GRIFFITH WILLIAMS

S.S. Marlene (London), Merchant Navy
who died age 23
on 4 April, 1941
Adopted son of Ellen Jane Jones, of Morfa Nevin,
Carnarvonshire
Remembered with honour

The S.S. Marlene was a 6,307 ton steam freighter which had been built in 1920 in Glasgow and was owned by Galraith Pembroke and Co. Ltd of London. She was on a voyage from Calcutta to the U.K. calling at Walrus Bay, South West Africa and Freetown with 8,700 tons of general cargo which included 1,300 tons of pig iron.

She was sunk just off the coast of West Africa by U-124 under the command of George-Willhelm Schulz. The submarine spotted the ship at 16.08 on the 4th April 1941 and immediately changed course to intercept. Four hours later the first torpedo was fired from under water. The torpedo, however, missed and the freighter which was now warned, changed course, went to full speed and commenced zigzagging while sending distress signals. At dusk visibility was reduced and Schulz decided to surface for a second attack. It took him another three hours to attain a new attack position.

At 23.02 a torpedo was fired which struck the Marlene amidships, right under the bridge but the ship still remained afloat. A third torpedo was fired at 23.28 which hit the ship abaft the mast. The ship still refused to sink and the U-boat commander decided upon an artillery attack opening fire with the deck gun, shelling Marlene with 12 rounds of incendiary shells.

Soon the ship was on fire but to every body's surprise the flames ceased. On 5th April at 00.05 a fourth torpedo was fired and finally the freighter slowly began to sink.

The master (Captain Henri Lascelles) and 46 of the crew landed at False Cape, Sierra Leone. Thirteen crew were lost and amongst them, unfortunately was young Edwin Griffith Williams. Edwin's home was Glan Morfa on the Nefyn road which was also the home of another young ship's carpenter (William Williams) who lost his life in the 1914-18 war.

The U-boat commander was decorated with Germany's highest honour, Knight's Cross (the highest Iron Cross classification). He lived in Hamburg where he died in 1986 at the age of 80.

George Willhelm Schulz

In Memory of
Carpenter THOMAS IDRIS JONES

S.S. Aguila (Liverpool), Merchant Navy
who died age 24
on 19 August, 1941
Son of Thomas and Mary Jones, of Morfa Nevin,
Carnarvonshire
Remembered with honour

NIGHTMARE CONVOY

IDRIS JONES – TAL Y LLYN

Idris Jones was the youngest of the four sons of Capt. and Mrs. Jones, Tal-y-Llyn, Morfa Nefyn. He joined the Merchant Navy in the early years of the war as a carpenter. In August 1941 he travelled to Liverpool to join his ship which turned out to be the Aguila, a 3,255 ton ship belonging to the Yeoward Line Ltd of Liverpool. The vessel had been built at Dundee in 1917 and in peacetime had operated as a cargo and passenger steamer trading mainly with the Canaries. She was fitted out with good accommodation for 150 passengers.

On this occasion, the Aguila was scheduled to call at Gibraltar and Lisbon with 397 bags of mail and some general cargo, together with 91 passengers. The passengers were mainly naval personnel who were travelling to Gibraltar to join ships or to be stationed on the Rock. Amongst them were 22 members of the W.R.N.S. who were the first batch of girls who had volunteered for cipher and wireless duties. This brought the total ship's compliment to 165 with Capt. Arthur Firth in command. Having been selected as the commodore ship for the convoy the Aguila had also on board Vice Admiral Patrick Perkins D.S.O. who would be in overall charge of the convoy.

The Aguila and five other ships left Liverpool on 13th August and met with 10 ships from Milford Haven and 6 from the Clyde to form convoy OG71 just off Belfast. The convoy proceeded via the North Channel round the North Coast of Ireland past Malin Head. After sailing well over to the west the convoy turned south, steaming parallel to the west coast of Ireland. From then on it was down to Gibraltar but executing a great curve to the west in order to keep a good distance from the coast of occupied France and avoiding spotter planes and U-boats.

The convoy was escorted by the 5th Escort Group of Naval vessels including the sloop Leith, destroyer Bath of the Royal Norwegian Navy, 6 corvettes and a trawler.

A pack of 8 U-Boats shadowed the convoy from as early as the 17th August managing to evade the escort ships which were continually making sweeps in search of them. A couple of the U-boats stealthily managed to overtake the convoy on the left flank and the events that followed in the early hours of the morning of 19th August turned out to be disastrous. At about 1 a.m. one U-boat surfaced and fired two torpedoes which struck HMS Bath tearing her in half and the ship sank in 3 minutes. At 1.35 a second merchant ship was hit and vanished beneath the waves.

Just after 3 a.m. U.201 under the command of Adalbert Schnee sank the British ship Ciscar. By this time Capt. Firth had ordered everyone on the Aguila to stand by with life jackets to be worn. However, within ten minutes two torpedoes struck the Aguila and she foundered in 90 seconds W.S.W. off Fastnet Rock in position 49 23N 17 36 W. Everything was so sudden that it was pure luck that 16 men survived. Capt. Firth and nine others were picked up by HMS Wallflower and landed at Gibraltar. Six crew members were rescued by the tug Royal Oak but later lost their lives when she in turn was sunk on the 22nd August. The convoy commodore, Vice Admiral Perkins, 65 crew members (amongst them Idris Jones) and 85 passengers including all the 22 WRNS lost their lives.

The convoy continued on its route to Gibraltar but was attacked again on the 22nd and 23rd of August and by the end of the voyage, out of the 22 ships in convoy 8 had been sunk together with two of the escorts with a loss of nearly 400 lives. Amongst the crew of one of the corvettes was the well known author Nicholas Monserrat. Commenting later about this convoy he said

"Whenever I think of the war I remember this convoy. It is my particular nightmare."

A lot of questions were asked as to why did it happen and what had gone wrong and a lengthy inquest was conducted entirely in secret. The conclusion that one reaches is that a catalogue of errors and a very successful German attack resulted in this disastrous episode in the war at sea. All the reasons and excuses however did not ease the pain and there was no compensation for Capt. and Mrs. Jones on the loss of their youngest son.

One interesting postscript to this sad story took place in 1951 when a new lifeboat was stationed at Aberystwyth. She was the gift of the "Aguila Wren" Memorial Fund and in the naming ceremony on June 28th 1952 the lifeboat was handed over by the father of one of the WRNS and named Aguila Wren by the mother of another of the 22 girls who lost their lives. Between 1951 and 1964 Aguila Wren was launched 21 times and saved 14 lives. In 1965 the boat was transferred to Redcar where she was launched 52 times and saved 36 lives. On the 20th May 1973 the boat was de-commissioned and handed over to the Sea Cadets at Scunthorpe.

Idris Jones with his older brother Griff (left)

The Liverpool steamer Aguila, *popular for her Canary Islands cruises, shortly before the outbreak of war.*

The lifeboat arrives at Aberystwyth

Adalbert Schnee

Returning to base after a successful operation

ANTARCTIC WHALING TO ARCTIC CONVOYS

CAPT. W. WILLIAMS – PRIMROSE VILLE

William Williams was born in 1888 at Tyn Parc, Rhiw on the Llŷn Peninsula. Although the son of a farmer young William had no interest in the land and his only ambition was to go to sea. With this in mind he left for London where he worked for a while with an uncle who owned a bakery. Whilst in London he studied seamanship at night school prior to embarking on his maritime career. Through hard work and diligent study he soon achieved his ambition to become a ship's officer eventually reaching the rank of Captain.

During the 1914-18 conflict the ship he was on was torpedoed but fortunately Capt. Williams and the crew members were rescued. The vessel which rescued them was a freighter named "Primrose Hill". This explains why the name Primrose eventually became the middle name of one of his twin daughters and Primrose Ville the name of one of the two houses he built in Lôn Las, Morfa Nefyn.

During his career Capt. Williams sailed to the Antarctic on numerous voyages many of them in command of his ship Southern King which belonged to the Southern Whaling and Sealing Company a subsidiary of Unilever Ltd. The Southern King was a supply ship which on the outward voyage conveyed passengers, coal and other vital supplies to South Georgia returning to the UK with whale oil and other products of the whaling industry such as baleen (whale bone).

By the 1930s Capt. Williams had become superintendent of the whaling company and he was instructed to recruit young Welsh men as whalers. The 1930s was a period of economic depression and a large percentage of the registered workforce in parts of rural Wales were unemployed. This was particularly true of Anglesey where Capt. Williams decided to concentrate his recruitment campaign. He set up his headquarters in Holyhead and in a very short time he engaged a total of forty four men who eventually left to join the two whaling factory ships Southern Empress and Southern Princess. They embarked from Newcastle in October 1936 calling at Las Palmas and Cape Town en route to the Antarctic. A well written book by Alun Owen provides an excellent insight into the life of "The Whalers of Anglesey" in the 1930s.

Capt. Williams as well as being a highly respected Master Mariner was also an astute observer of everything he saw during his travels. Through his interest in photography he was able to record these observations and I am grateful to the family for allowing me to reproduce some of the excellent prints of South Georgia in the 1930s.

Following the decline in whaling and the onset of the Second World War, Capt. Williams made his contribution to the war effort by taking command of one of the "Empire" ships as they were known. These were ships built during the war for the British Ministry of Shipping. A considerable number were built and each one was given the prefix – Empire. These ships were employed to convey supplies to strategic areas involving considerable danger and a high risk of attack from the enemy. 196 Empire ships were sunk during W.W.2 and amongst them was the Empire Gilbert with Capt. Williams in command. The vessel was a steam freighter of 6,640 tons built in 1941 and on this fateful voyage was conveying essential equipment to Russia via the Arctic.

The route to the Russian ports of Archangel and Murmansk was particularly vulnerable to attack by aircraft, submarines and surface vessels, since for a considerable distance it passed within range of enemy occupied Norway. Moreover, the winter conditions were among the worst to be encountered anywhere and in summer the perpetual daylight increased the danger of observation and successful attack. A maritime historian wrote

> "Nowhere was courage shown under conditions of such prolonged strain, seemingly adverse odds of intense climatic discomfort as on the convoy routes to North Russia."

The Empire Gilbert left the Tyne in October 1942 calling at Loch Ewe and Reykjavik before progressing to Archangel. Most ships taking this dangerous route did so in convoy but a few ships did travel alone thinking that stealth would get them through. This was the case with the Empire Gilbert but unfortunately she was spotted east of Iceland by U-boat 586 under the command of Dietrich Von Der Esch. The U-boat had left Skjomenfjord in Norway on Oct 11th and returned there three and a half weeks later on 5th November having sunk the Empire Gilbert on the 2nd November 1942.

Capt. Williams and all but two of the crew lost their lives in these icy waters and ironically the German U-boat commander also lost his life when his U-boat was sunk on 5th July 1944 near Toulon after being attacked by an American B.24 aircraft.

The name of Capt Williams is inscribed on the Tower Hill Memorial and it was a proud if sad moment for Margaret Williams and her sister when they attended the unveiling ceremony on the 5th November 1955. Ten years earlier an extract in the London Gazette read as follows.

> "For great bravery and devotion to duty in
> carrying supplies to North Russia"
>
> Mentioned in Dispatches (Posthumous)
> Capt. William Williams, Master, Merchant Navy.

A fitting epitaph to a very gallant mariner.

In Memory of
Master WILLIAM WILLIAMS

S.S. Empire Gilbert (Sunderland), Merchant Navy
who died age 54
on 02 November 1942
Husband of M. Williams of Morfa Nevin, Caernarvonshire.
Remebered with honour
TOWER HILL MEMORIAL

Southern King – Capt. Williams' ship

Capt. W. Williams on Deck

In the jaws of the whale

South Georgia Whaling Station. The ship in the picture is the Southern King.

King Penguins

Seals

Albatross

Whale Catchers

Harpoon Gun

Capt. Williams – with Norwegian Flensers

Flensers at work – a form of filleting

THE MERCHANT NAVY MEMORIAL
ON
TOWER HILL

Admit Bearer to
THE RELATIVES ENCLOSURE
at the
CEREMONY OF UNVEILING
by
HER MAJESTY THE QUEEN
on Saturday, 5th November, 1955

TICKET HOLDERS MUST BE IN THEIR PLACES BY 1.45 P.M.

SEE OVER

Dietrich von der Esch
Born on31 Jan, 1915 in Berlin-Carlottenburg.
Crew 34. Kapitänleutnant (1 Apr, 1942)
Died on 29 Sep, 1944, South Atlantic.

Commands:
U-586, U-606, U-863

RESCUED BY THE ROYAL NAVY

CAPT. SAMUEL K. WILLIAMS – IVY DALE

Sam Williams was the son of Capt. and Mrs. Williams Ivy Dale, Lôn Bridin, Morfa Nefyn. Both he and his brother John followed in their father's footsteps and became mariners. Sam as a young teenager travelled to Tyneside to join his first ship the S.S. North Anglia as an Ordinary Seaman. The North Anglia (3,562 tons) was a tramp steamer belonging to the company owned and managed by Hugh Roberts and Son of Newcastle. The company had very close local connections since Hugh Roberts was a native of Edern and many of the masters and crew employed by him were from the Llŷn Peninsula.

In the interwar years Sam served on a variety of ships and travelled all over the world gaining valuable experience. He twice circumnavigated the world, experienced a hurricane in the Caribbean and was bombed in Spain during the Civil War. He also managed to find time to study and add qualifications to his practical experience. By the onset of war he had qualified for his 1st Mate Certificate and by 1942 had obtained his Master's certificate.

In that year he was employed by the United Africa Company (a subsidiary of Unilever) which had considerable trading interests in West Africa. He was appointed as Chief Officer on one of a number of coastal vessels which the company owned and which traded along the West African coast and up the many creeks and rivers in the area. Sam left the UK on Friday 18th December 1942 serving as an extra Chief Officer on the S.S. Zarian en route to Lagos in Nigeria where he would take up his new appointment.

The Zarian, a freighter of 4,871 tons left Leith with a cargo of general and government stores, a crew of 42, 7 gunners and 4 passengers. She progressed to Loch Ewe where she joined 44 other merchant ships to form convoy ONS 154. The "O" signified that this convoy was outward bound from the U.K. the "N" showed the destination was North America, while the "S" indicated that this was a slow convoy, not capable of maintaining a speed above 10 knots. The Zarian would obviously have left the convoy in the Atlantic to progress un-escorted to West Africa.

The merchant ships were escorted by the Royal Canadian Navy escort group C1 consisting of five corvettes, a rescue ship and a tanker assigned to refuel the escort vessels at sea. The destroyer H.M.C.S. St. Laurent joined the group just west of Ireland. This was a relatively small escort group for such a large convoy which was spread over an area 5 miles wide and 1.5 miles deep. The winter of 1942/43 was one of the "most ferocious winters in living memory" and the ships encountered very heavy seas in the Western Approaches. On Sunday, December 22nd U356 attacked the convoy and torpedoed 6 ships before she herself was sunk by the destroyer St. Laurent.

The main attack came on the night of December 28th/29th when 19 U-boats in two wolf packs attacked the convoy. This was a system developed by the Germans which involved U-boats in patrol lines scouting for convoys. Once a convoy was spotted the first boat was designated "shadower" and would chase the convoy and report its heading and speed allowing other boats to form around it and attack more or less at will. usually on the surface at night. This is what happened to ONS 154 and in a two hour period 9 more ships were sunk or damaged including the Zarian. Samuel Williams in later years wrote a graphic account of his own experience during this attack and I am including part of it in the paragraphs that follow.

"The number of our ship in the convoy was 13 which meant we were the 3rd ship in the first column on the left flank of the convoy and in a very vulnerable position. When our side of the convoy was attacked the first ship to be hit was number 11 followed by 12 and it was obvious our turn next. I was certain I had seen a submarine and was in the act of raising my binoculars to have a better look when the torpedo hit the engine room with a terrific explosion. Every component part shook and trembled and the stern on which I stood was whipping about in a crazy manner. I waded along the decks which were awash only to find that the boats on the port side had been completely shattered by the force of the explosion. The only existing boat was already in the water and filled to capacity. There was no room for those of us who were still left on the ship. The rafts were our only hope of salvation. I proceeded to the Main Mast rigging followed by six others, only to find that the releasing gear had jammed. We worked like Trojans in a frenzy of desperation to release the raft. After a mighty effort, it slid over the side, followed by a splash. Then we followed by lowering ourselves into the icy waters of the North Atlantic.

The struggle for survival completely eliminated any sense of suffering. We were fully clad and wearing kapok lifejackets to which was attached a small red light. I struck out boldly for the raft and reached it in record time. I felt quite fresh and clambered on to the raft; a young l ad followed and joined me. We could see little red lights that represented our shipmates bobbing up and down in the water. I shouted encouragement and slowly one by one they reached the raft. We heaved them on board and they lay exhausted on the bottom. There were two brothers among them. One was the Chief Engineer of the ship; and the other was also a Chief Engineer going out to West Africa to join the same ship as myself. The Chief Engineer was the last to be hauled aboard our raft our refuge from the might and fury of the Atlantic Ocean.

A gentle, but cold wind made us realise how wet and cold we were. We busied ourselves in making conditions more comfortable and tolerable on the raft. The canvas dodger was rigged to keep off the wind and we took stock of the situation. The lifeboat lay nearby. We kept in touch by shouting across to each other. Presently, a dark shape loomed out of the darkness, we silently watched and wondered. It began to assume a definite form. By jove, yes, it was a submarine, silently gliding past us. A faint ripple was discernable where her bow should be and her conning tower was boldly sticking out of the water, whether we had been observed or not we couldn't say. She was proceeding in the direction of the convoy that was lit up on the horizon like Piccadilly Circus. The shells and the rockets were still being fired. We hoped that one of our escorts would catch her but I never did hear if any of the submarines had been sunk. How many seamen perished that awful night is hard to say. We lost four of our crew. The raft heaved and groaned to the moderate swell throughout the night. Sleep was out of the question. Rescue was paramount in our thoughts and we were mainly silent, each man preoccupied with his own thoughts. The dawn would perhaps solve our problems. the dawn had hardly broken when a British destroyer came in sight. We signalled SOS, which she acknowledged with a welcome OK. In no time, we found solid decks under our feet again."

The U-boats had outnumbered the escorts three to one and infiltrated the convoy at will inflicting horrendous losses. 14 merchant ships were lost in the battle and 510 sailors perished.

The Zarian had been attacked just after 11.00 p.m. on the night of the 28th December and was so badly damaged that the crew had to abandon ship. The vessel, however, did not sink until she was torpedoed again the following day. The initial attack had been made by U406 under the command of Horst Dietrichs and the end came when a torpedo was fired from U591 commanded by Hans Jurgen Zetzsche.

When Sam Williams was rescued by the destroyer HMS Milne he was very well treated by the officers of that ship who supplied him with a clean shirt and a pair of trousers enabling him to clean and dry his own clothes which were wet and badly stained with fuel oil. H.M.S. Milne took the survivors to Ponta Delgada in the Azores which they reached on the afternoon of January 1st. There were a large number of survivors in the port and the troopship Llangibby Castle arrived on January 6th to take them all back to Britain. Sam, however, was determined to get to West Africa and was very fortunate that HMS Milne had berthed next to a naval corvette HMS Petunia which was due to embark for Freetown in Sierra Leone and Sam and his Chief Engineer companion requested a passage on her and this was granted. A day after HMS Petunia left the Azores, however, she was diverted to Gibraltar and it was here that Sam was fitted out with survivor kits and spent a pleasant evening ashore. The following day he was ordered to report on a vessel which was about to sail for Freetown. This was a C.A.M.S. ship namely a Catapult Armed Merchant Ship. There were about 35 of these ships in service all having been fitted with a rocket propelled trolley which carried a Hurricane fighter on a catapult fitted in the bows of the ship. The pilot of this plane could not return to the ship but would ditch his aircraft in the sea hoping that he would be picked up. It was not a very successful idea although these ships made 175 voyages during which 12 were sunk and only 8 catapult launches were made, 6 enemy aircraft were shot down and one RAF pilot died.

The voyage to West Africa was uneventful and at last Sam Williams had reached his destination where he remained for the next few years eventually taking command of his own vessel.

When his tour of duty expired he returned to the UK and in February 1947 he joined the M.V. Empire Tagamax in Avonmouth The ship renamed the Busen Star was employed in the whaling industry conveying fuel oil and supplies to the whalers in Antarctica and returning to the UK with whale oil. Sam made numerous voyages to Antarctica and most of them in command of his own ship until he eventually retired. His had been an exciting and successful career which started when he and his brother John used to spend hours in their small rowing boat "Carry me Safe" which was always berthed at Bwlch Porthdinllaen.

A/B Williams

2nd Mate Williams

Captain Samuel K. Williams

One of the Escort Ships to Convoy ONS 154

C.A.M.S. Ship

I COME FROM MORFA NEFYN

DEWI EVANS – MONEIFION

Dewi Evans was the son of Capt. and Mrs. David Evans of Moneifion, Lôn Penrhos. He went to sea in 1934 joining the S.S. Menestheus at Liverpool as a Deck Boy. The voyages on this vessel took him to Japan and other Far Eastern destinations. The Menestheus was built in 1929 for the Ocean S.S. Co. (Blue Funnel Line) to be employed on their Liverpool – Far East service. In 1940 she became a naval minelayer and in 1943 was converted to a naval recreation ship (for the Pacific Fleet). Seamen took their local leave aboard her and she was fitted with a cinema/theatre, swimming pool and brewery. In 1946 she left Yokohama for the U.K. to be de-commissioned and in 1948 was returned to her owners and commercial service. In April 1953 an explosion in the engine room resulted in a severe fire off the coast of California. She had to be abandoned and later towed to Long Beach and scrapped – a sad end for a fine ship.

Dewi had two years ashore following these voyages but with the outbreak of war in 1939 he resumed his maritime career, sailing from Liverpool, Cardiff and Hull to West Africa and other destinations. In August 1940 he joined the "City of Sydney" as a Junior Engineer serving in this capacity for two voyages both of which were fortunately uneventful. In April 1941 he transferred to a sister ship "City of Winchester" again as an engineer. The ship which was a 7,240 ton freighter left London in late April en route for Table Bay and Beira in Mozambique with a general cargo and a crew of 97. After leaving the Thames estuary the "City of Winchester" and numerous other vessels formed convoy OB313 and proceeded south in the Atlantic keeping west of the Canary Islands. On the evening of the 9th May 1941 the ship was struck by a torpedo in position 08 20N/26 14W. Two days later another City ship in the convoy the City of Shanghai was also sunk. Both vessels were victims to the same U-boat (U103) which was under the command of one of Germany's leading submariners – Victor Schutze. The U 103 under his command left Lorient in France on 1st April 1941 and returned there fourteen and a half weeks later on 12th July 1941. During this patrol alone the U-boat destroyed 13 ships and as a result Victor Schutze was awarded the Knight's Cross with Oak leaves. In his career as a submariner he destroyed 35 merchant ships. He survived the war but died in Frankfurt in 1950 at the relatively young age of 44.

Following the terrific explosion when the torpedo hit the ship, Dewi, who was in his cabin at the time, reported to the Chief Engineer who immediately instructed him to report on deck to prepare for abandoning ship. On reaching the deck, Dewi reported to his emergency station and involved himself in assisting with lowering the lifeboats. Fortunately, there was time for an orderly operation and all the crew, apart from 6, who had been killed in the original explosion, managed to safely board one of the ship's rescue boats.

Dewi found himself in a boat under the command of the 2nd mate from the ship, a gentlemen whom he had not met previously. After a few hours, when things had settled down, Dewi found himself in the stern of the boat sitting next to the 2nd mate and they got into conversation with each other. The mate turned to Dewi and said "I believe you're a Taffy" – the reply was emphatic – "Yes and very proud of the fact.". "Where do you come from in Wales?" – "Caernarfonshire". "Where in Caernarfonshire?" – "A small village called Morfa Nefyn". At this the mate seemed quite amazed and so was Dewi when he said – "I'm living in Nefyn now and my wife is from Morfa Nefyn."

It transpired that 2nd Mate Ralph Hewitt Bellhouse whose family was connected in some way with the Cliff Castle, Nefyn, had married Rosalind McCurdy of Cairn Nevis, Lôn Uchaf. Rosalind died in 1963 but Ralph, who eventually became a Captain, survived her and died in 1975. Their daughter Patricia died 4 years later. All share the same grave in the local churchyard.

Unfortunately for Dewi and the rest of the crew in the lifeboat the prevailing tide and currents were not helpful and for over a week the boat drifted one way and then another. The weather, however, was good and the sea reasonably calm but the men were feeling the effects of having very little to eat and drink in the restricted space of the lifeboat. Just as things were getting quite serious they were fortunately spotted on the 10th day by a Norwegian freighter that took them to the West African port of Takoradi. From there they were escorted to Accra to await a ship for the return journey to the U.K.

In Accra the men were put up in a small hotel and it was while resting here that Dewi was summoned from his room to the reception area to meet a Mr. and Mrs. Evans. He went downstairs slowly thinking someone was playing a joke on him but was surprised to discover that a Mr. and Mrs. Evans were there to greet him. It transpired that Mr. Evans was the Welsh Manager of a West African gold mine and he and his wife were anxious to help sailors (in this case, their Welsh namesake) who had lost everything apart from the clothes they were wearing. They were extremely kind to Dewi who was allowed to accompany them to their home where he stayed for 3 days before having to report back to board a ship for the U.K. On returning to Cardiff Dewi spent some time convalescing in hospital before returning home to Morfa Nefyn wearing the clothes the Evans family had kindly given him.

Dewi Evans

Dewi Evans

The first ship Dewi Evans sailed on.

Victor Schutze

CAPTURED ON THE HIGH SEAS

CAPT. EVAN DAVIES – HAFAN

Capt. Evan Davies lived at Hafan (now Clwyd), Lôn Las, Morfa Nefyn, with his wife and three sons. He was the son of Terfyn, Morfa Nefyn and his father Capt. Robert Davies was a well known local master mariner and was Captain of the schooner "Polly Preston".

Evan Davies went to sea at an early age, served throughout the 1st World War and gained his master's certificate whilst still relatively young. In the interwar years he sailed all over the world and when hostilities broke out in 1939 he was 50 years old and contemplating retirement. In 1941, however, he took command of the M.V. Dalhousie, which was berthed in the Surrey docks, London. She was a diesel vessel of 9,200 tons which had only been launched in August 1940 at a cost of £130,000. Built to peacetime standards, she represented the very latest in British tramp shipping and was a very fine modern cargo ship.

The Dalhousie was well armed for a merchant ship, having a 4" gun and a Bofors aft, two Oerlikons at the after end of the boatdeck, two Hotchkiss on the bridge, rockets on each side of the boat deck and depth charges aft. Although the merchant sailors formed the nucleus of the gun crews a number of naval personnel had also been allocated to the ship. Her managing owner was a Greek, named Nicholaides, who paid wages above the standard rates and ensured the ship was well found – he was in partnership with an Englishman named Gundry.

The Dalhousie left the Clyde on what turned out to be her final voyage in 1942. The cargo which included a tank landing craft was scheduled for Port Said. The outward voyage via Cape Town, Aden, the Red Sea to Port Said was relatively uneventful. The planned route for the return leg was via Aden and Cape Town across the Atlantic to Trinidad and on to Houston in Texas and then in convoy to the U.K.

After bunkering in Cape Town, Capt. Davies set course for Trinidad. All was well until they were in mid-Atlantic when the lookout on the bridge noticed a vessel on the horizon that at first glance appeared to be a small merchantman. When the small ship started firing Capt. Davies immediately realised that she was a German raider in disguise. The Dalhousie was manoeuvred into position for her 4" gun to be used but the firing power of the raider was much greater. Within a short time a number of shells hit the Dalhousie badly damaging and setting the ship on fire. Another ship appeared on the horizon and the German ship ordered Capt. Davies to stop and abandon the vessel. He had no option but to comply with the request as there was no escape. When the lifeboats were in the water the German vessel came nearer and instructed the boats to pull up alongside for the crew to climb aboard. Fortunately there was no loss of life. Following this, more gun fire resulted in the Dalhousie sinking and Capt. Davies and his crew were prisoners aboard the German raider "Stier". All this happened on August 9th 1942 in position 22º24'S, 24º 50'W.

The Steir was a 4,418 ton ship – formerly the "Cairo" from the Deutche – Levante Line. On May 12th 1942 under Capt. Horst Gerlach she shipped out of Rotterdam and sailed down the English Channel into the Atlantic. She was fired on by shore batteries from Dover, and attacked by motor torpedo boats but managed to run the gauntlet. She sank her first ship "Gemstone" on June 4th and two days later an American merchantman "Stanvac Calcutta" – Capt. Gerlach spent the next two months patrolling in the Atlantic and was joined by another raider "Michel". Success evaded them and they decided to part company and meet again on August 9th. The Stier came across the Dalhousie only a matter of hours before the Michel arrived at their rendezvous.

Life as prisoners on board the Stier was not too bad and Capt. Davies found himself berthed with other officers in a large room with a couple of tables and benches, double tiered bunks and a few lockers. The men were allowed on deck once a day for exercise and the food was more than adequate. The Stier sailed south, with the weather fine and fresh and when close to one of the Tristan da Cunha group of islands she met up with a large supply ship called the Charlotte Schlieman. The meeting was to enable the prisoners to be transferred to the larger vessel. This took place in an orderly manner but Capt. Davies and one other were allowed to remain on the Stier and were joined by a Capt. Griffiths who had been in command of the Gemstone. All the prisoners who were transferred ended up in Japan as prisoners of war.

Following this stop the Stier passed round the Tristan de Cunah islands and then headed north to rendezvous with the supply ship Tannenfels on September 27th. As she was approaching the new rendezvous she was surprised by the American Liberty ship Stephen Hawkins en route from Cape Town to Bahia. Because of fog the adversaries did not see each other until they were about 2 miles apart. Stier opened fire at 08.54 and quickly reduced the American Ship to a hulk. The Hawkins, however, hit back with her single 4" gun and hit Stier 13 times including two shots that knocked out her steering gear and started a fire in the engine room at 09.05 Stier ceased fire at 09.18 and the Stephen Hawkins sank at 10.00. With his own ship ablaze, Capt. Gerlach gave the order to abandon ship and Stier sank at about 11.40. All this time Capt. Davies and the other prisoners had been in a lock up directly under the focsle head gun. They were released but Capt. Davies had been overcome by smoke and fumes and was half carried up on deck by his two companions. He also badly damaged his shoulder when he fell against a ladder. The three of them managed to seize a rubber raft and got over the side with many other crew members and were eventually picked up by the Tannenfels. On board there was already over 300 men and prisoners with only sufficient provisions to last this compliment for 3 weeks. Now she had an extra large number from the raider. In order to avoid capture she sailed south and it took seven weeks before she reached Bordeaux in France. Living conditions were dreadful with very little to eat. Capt. Davies was transferred from the ship on to cattle trucks which conveyed him and the other sailors to the prisoner of war camp Mimlag-Nord a few miles north of Bremen in Germany. By this time Capt. Davies weighed only 6 stone.

He was released in 1945 and returned to Morfa Nefyn where he lived until his death in 1966.

Above – "Dalhousie"
Capt. Davies' Ship

Capt. Horst Gerlach

Below – German Raider "Stier"

"Stier" disguised as a peaceful merchantsman

Dalhousie sinking.
Stier on the left.
Picture taken from the other raider "Michel"

The badly damaged "Stier" on fire in several places.

WAR TIME HEROISM

CAPT. J. LEWIS JONES – HIGHWAYS

John Lewis Jones was better known to those who were at school with him as Jack Plisman because his father was for many years the popular village policeman at Nefyn. Morfa Nefyn people would know him as Jack "Highways" after the name of the family home in Lôn Uchaf. On leaving Pwllheli County School in 1937 Jack embarked on a maritime career and joined his first ship in North Shields as a sixteen year old apprentice. The ship was a tanker called San Felix and during the voyage of 9 _ months they visited places like Rio de Janeiro, Montevideo and Buenos Aires before returning to Birkenhead.

After a short spell of leave Jack joined another tanker belonging to the Eagle Oil and Shipping Company. The name of this ship was the "San Demetrio" and Jack was to remain with her for almost two years. The ship made numerous voyages from the Gulf of Mexico ports to the U.K. with petroleum and this continued after hostilities were declared in September 1939. On 28th October 1940 the ship joined 38 other merchant ships to form convoy HX84 departing from Halifax, Nova Scotia for the U.K. Once outside Canadian waters the only escort the convoy had was the Armed Merchant Cruiser H.M.S. Jarvis Bay which was armed with seven old 6" guns and an out of date fire control system. The Jarvis Bay was an old 14,164 ton passenger liner built in 1922 and used to carry immigrants to Australia and food back to Britain. In 1939 along with another 56 passenger liners she was converted into an AMC. She was under the command of Capt. E.S.F. Fegen R.N. with a crew of 254 – a mixture of both R.N. and Merchant Navy personnel.

On 27th October 1940 the German Pocket Battleship the "Admiral Scheer" commanded by Capt. Theodore Krank, left Kiel and after a short stop in Stavanger, Norway, managed to break out into the North Atlantic. Kranke was informed by German Intelligence that Convoy HX84 had left Halifax and was ordered to intercept it and destroy as many ships as he could. As the Admiral Scheer got close to the escorted ships a float plane was launched which soon spotted the convoy and was able to report its speed, heading and position.

Capt. Kranke went to full speed to intercept and at twilight on the 5th November the convoy was sited.

This was when the Jarvis Bay spotted a ship on the horizon but did not realise it was the Admiral Scheer until the enemy turned broadside and fired her six 11" guns. Immediately the convoy was ordered to scatter and Capt. Fegan turned the Jarvis Bay at full speed ahead towards the enemy dropping smoke floats as they went. The German ship soon got the range and 11" shells started to rip the Jarvis Bay apart bit by bit. The ship however continued on a course direct at the Admiral Scheer firing its outdated 6" guns and for 22 minutes this one-sided battle continued until eventually the Jarvis Bay was sunk with a loss of 189 lives. With valuable minutes and 385 shells spent on the destruction of the Jarvis Bay, the Scheer gave chase to the now scattered convoy. The slowest ships were the first caught and sunk including the S.S. Beaverford (10,042 tons) sunk with a loss of 77 lives, the S.S. Kinbane Head (5,225 tons) – 24 lives, S.S. Maiden (7,908 tons) – 91 lives, S.S. Trewelland (5,201 tons) – 16 lives, S.S. Vigaland – 12 lives. A total of 440 lives were lost in the attack but 32 ships had escaped and countless lives were saved, all because of the gallant actions of the Jarvis Bay. Captain Fegen was posthumously awarded the Victoria Cross for his bravery. The San Demetrio by this time was steaming away from the raider but still in the line of fire. Very soon the "Scheer" concentrated her fire on the tanker and after numerous hits, fierce fires broke out amidship and aft and owing to the volatile nature of the cargo the vessel was abandoned. Jack's lifeboat was the first to be launched. Sixteen of the crew were in the boat and they rowed for their lives away from the burning vessel in case it exploded. The time was approximately 17.30 and the German raider continued firing until about midnight.

In the early hours of the 5th of November, the wind freshened from the south-west and blew a full gale, with very high seas and swell. The men were now fighting for survival as the sea swamped the boat and they had to bail for their lives. A few hours after daybreak a vessel was sighted about 4 miles away and in spite of firing red flares they could not attract her attention.

Later that afternoon a second ship was sighted to windward. The men hoisted a main sail and jib and sailed to meet the vessel arriving close to her just before dark. After a while and to their amazement they realised it was their own ship still burning and helpless. It was decided that it would be foolish to attempt to board her at that time and so they decided to lay off on her weather side until next morning.

The sail was lowered and the sea anchor set and a canvas dodger placed round the lifeboat's bow as protection from the wind and the sea. The weather worsened and torrential rain added to the men's discomfort and all were suffering from cold and exposure. Calum McNeil, a sailor from the Isle of Barra, describes an incident which happened during the night

"Suddenly a light shone overhead and a shout of 'A plane, a plane' went up. We burnt a flare, we signalled with a torch and all was hustle and scurry. Then from the stern we heard young Jones's quiet voice saying. 'That is no plane, that's bloody Jupiter.' He was right. Bloody Jupiter it was".

That night passed very slowly and a short while after dawn broke San Demetrio was again sighted about 5 miles away. The sail was set again and they were close alongside her by noon.

The rest of this account is as it was written by Jack himself:

"She was still on fire, but no one objected to reboarding, which was soon successfully accomplished. Anything was better than remaining in the lifeboat, and it was obvious that further time spent in the boat was going to be a futile attempt to survive. We were only partially successful in recovering our life-boat, which was left hanging in the falls about six feet clear of the sea.

From the boat it was seen that the ship was badly damaged; after boarding, the damage found was appalling. A shell had entered the port bow just above the waterline, exploded, and splinters had holed our collision bulkhead, resulting in our forehold making water which was settling the vessel by the head. The bridge and all midship accommodation was a mass of twisted steel, the main deck under the structure was buckled with heat from the fire, which had been so intense that the brass and glass of the portholes had melted and fused, resembling icicles. Part of this mess was still burning.

The main deck abaft the bridge had a number of splinter holes, and the petrol cargo was flooding from this as the ship rolled.

All the accommodation on the port side had been destroyed, also the decks. This area was still on fire.

These fires were attacked with fire extinguishers and buckets to begin with, and with fire hoses when the Chief Engineer raised sufficient steam to operate the pumps. The fires were extinguished in about five hours.

It was now dark, and as nothing further could be accomplished, watches were set for the night. Four cabins were intact and all enjoyed a few hours of luxurious sleep.

The weather worsened during the night and the insecured life-boat was lost. The fire aft broke out again, but was extinguished by the watch on deck. Now that our life-boat had gone, we had no choice but to remain aboard. During the forenoon on the 8th November all hands were employed in plugging the splinter holes in the main deck and salvaging any food, etc. remaining. We had ample potatoes and onions and a little condensed milk. The freezer was full of ready-cooked meat, thanks to the fire, but inedible as it was found to be contaminated with ammonia. Three bottles of rum were also found, a most welcome discovery. During the afternoon the Chief Engineer announced that his engines would operate. We had nothing left to navigate with, but if we shaped a course to the west we were bound to make the coast of the United Sates or Canada and safety. This would entail heading into the weather, and with the damage forward it was considered the ship would probably sink. This left no alternative but to head eastward, hoping to reach the coast of Ireland or Scotland, running with the weather on our stern. Our progress eastward began during the afternoon. We navigated by rare glimpses of the sun and stars, but mainly by keeping the wind astern.

The 9th November to 12th November we proceeded approximately eastward in very heavy weather, the vessel labouring and becoming very sluggish. To relieve the situation, cargo was gravitated from the forward tank to amidships, and this helped. Though the weather was causing grave concern regarding remaining afloat, it was so bad that submarines would not be active had we been sighted in the poor visibility. In this respect the weather was in our favour.

On the 13th November, land was sighted in the forenoon. We hoped it to be Ireland, but it could easily have been occupied France. We sighted a bay and entered, laying there the night.

Early on the 14th November an aircraft flew overhead, and soon a vessel approached which was a British tug. Later, the destroyer H.M.S. Arrow came to our aid. At 18.30 we proceeded towards the Clyde escorted by the destroyer, which was later joined by others; we were also given continuous air cover during daylight. I doubt that any single merchant ship had up to that time enjoyed such a strong escorting force. The San Demetrio anchored in the Clyde on the 16th November. The greatest satisfaction to Mr. Pollard, our Chief Engineer, was to be able to discharge the cargo through the ship's pipes with her own pumping equipment and that 11,000 tons of the original 11,200 tons with which she had sailed was saved. Compared to present-day cargoes of 500,000 tons, perhaps not a large quantity, but every drop was precious at that time.

I left the vessel a few days later. Similar incidents were often to be repeated during the next five years, particularly in 1943 when the Battle of the Atlantic reached its climax. Further ships in which I served and left, and hundreds more, San Demetrio among them, were later lost. Many friends of mine were lost with them.

I consider myself very fortunate to have survived the war years and been able to continue with my sea career until 1971, latterly in a relieving capacity, whereas many friends hardly got the chance to begin theirs."

J. Lewis Jones

The events in the Atlantic caused great concern to everyone locally and it was very worrying times for Mr and Mrs. Jones especially when they received a letter dated 13th November from the Eagle

Oil and Shipping Company stating that there was no news of Jack and the other 15 crew members. It was joy and relief when the news eventually came that the 16 men had recovered the ship and sailed her back to the U.K. ensuring that the name of the San Demetrio was written firmly into the history of the Merchant Navy.

POSTSCRIPTS

1. Extracts from the London Gazette

SECOND SUPPLEMENT
TO
THE LONDON GAZETTE
of FRIDAY, the 21st of FEBRUARY 1941
TUESDAY, 25th FEBRUARY 1941

Awarded the Medal of the Civil Division of the
Most Excellent Order of the British Empire
for Meritorious Service
John Lewis Jones, Apprentice. S.S. San Demetrio

He kept alternate watches and was of the utmost help when navigating the vessel without books instruments, charts or compasses. He showed spirit and courage throughout. He immediately volunteered to go down to the pump room with the Chief Engineer and open the valves although it was full of gas. In every other way he proved willing and resourceful and showed himself to be an admirable Second in Command.

The ship, with most of her valuable cargo was brought into port.

LLOYDS WAR MEDAL
FOR
BRAVERY AT SEA
THIRD LIST OF AWARDS

Apprentice Jones helped to navigate the vessel without books, instruments, charts or compass. He kept alternate watches. He was one of those who offered to accompany the chief engineer to the gas-filled pump room. He proved a most capable second-in-command. It was mainly due to the efforts of the chief engineer and Apprentice Jones that the ship was brought into port and most of her valuable cargo saved.

2. Calum McNeil and another able seaman from the San Demetrio, Roddie MacLennan, went home on leave to their native island of Barra in the Outer Hebrides to find there an acute shortage

of whisky. However, early in December S.S. Politician with a cargo, mostly of whisky, ran aground in thick fog to the north of Barra. The islanders went out in their small boats and there was "Whisky Galore" for MacLennan's wedding later that month. (Remember the film).

3. In 1943 a film "San Demetrio, London" was produced by Michael Balcon at Ealing Studios in London. The cast included many well known film stars of the period including Walter Fitzgerald, Ralph Michael, Gordon Jackson, Mervyn Johns and Barry Letts as young Apprentice Jones.

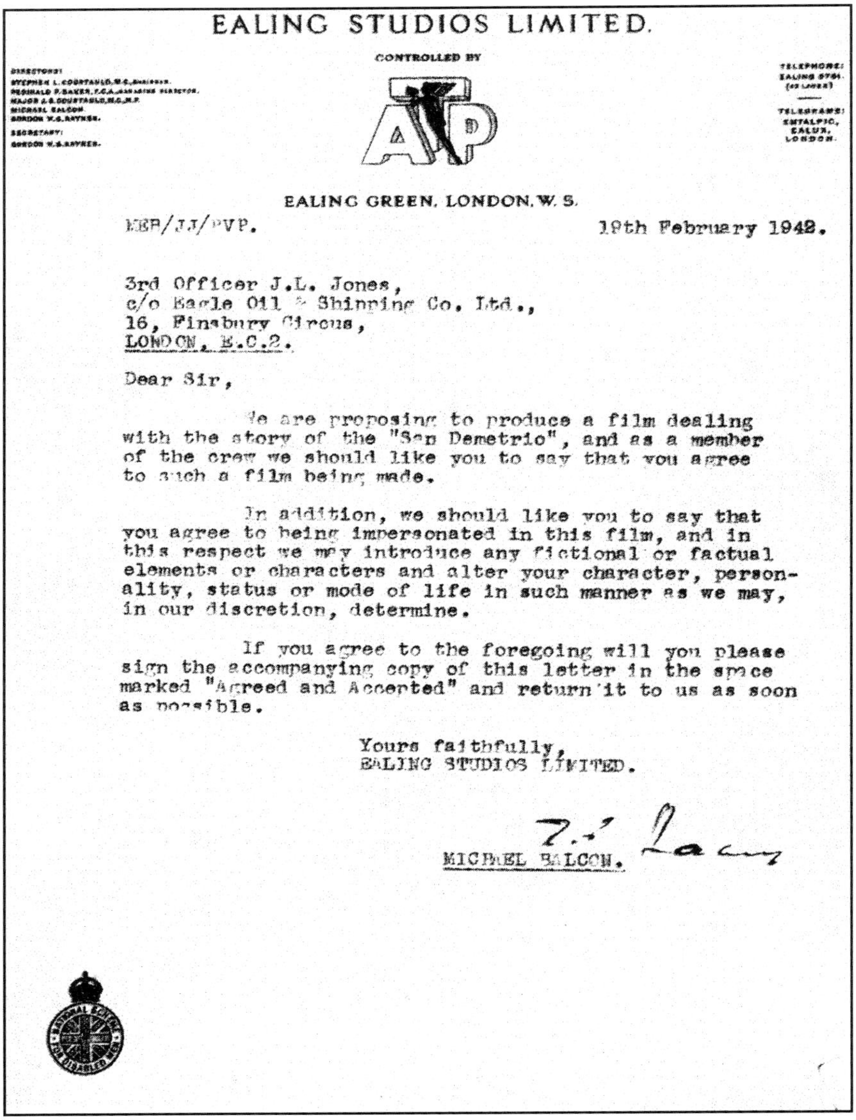

EALING STUDIOS LIMITED.

CONTROLLED BY

ATP

DIRECTORS:
STEPHEN L. COURTAULD, M.C., Chairman.
REGINALD P. BAKER, F.C.A., Managing Director.
MAJOR J. S. COURTAULD, M.C., M.P.
MICHAEL BALCON.
GORDON W. S. RAYNES.

SECRETARY:
GORDON W. S. RAYNES.

TELEPHONE:
EALING 6761.
(12 LINES)

TELEGRAMS:
ENTALPIC,
EALUX,
LONDON.

EALING GREEN, LONDON, W. 5.

MEB/JJ/PVP. 19th February 1942.

3rd Officer J.L. Jones,
c/o Eagle Oil & Shipping Co. Ltd.,
16, Finsbury Circus,
LONDON, E.C.2.

Dear Sir,

We are proposing to produce a film dealing with the story of the "San Demetrio", and as a member of the crew we should like you to say that you agree to such a film being made.

In addition, we should like you to say that you agree to being impersonated in this film, and in this respect we may introduce any fictional or factual elements or characters and alter your character, personality, status or mode of life in such manner as we may, in our discretion, determine.

If you agree to the foregoing will you please sign the accompanying copy of this letter in the space marked "Agreed and Accepted" and return it to us as soon as possible.

Yours faithfully,
EALING STUDIOS LIMITED.

MICHAEL BALCON.

Apprentice J. L. Jones

Capt. E.S.E. Fegen

Theodore Kranke

EAGLE OIL & SHIPPING COMPANY LIMITED.

LONDON.

MAIL No

Langdon Court,
Wembury,
near Plymouth.

FH/AMcE-12.

Mr. R. Jones,
Police Station,
Nevin, Caerns.

13th November, 1940.

Dear Sir,

In reply to your enquiry of the 9th inst. we regret to have to inform you that the ship in which your son was serving has been lost by enemy action, but all of the crew managed to get away safely in the boats.

At the time of writing the Master and 23 of the crew have arrived safely at St. Johns, Newfoundland, but the second boat (in charge of the 2nd Officer and Chief Engineer) has not yet reported. Your son is in this boat. We are sorry not to be able, as yet, to give you news of his safety but as the boat is well found in every way and in charge of experienced men, and as the weather was fine at the time, we have every hope that we shall shortly have news of the safety of all the men. Needless to say we will let you know immediately we have further news.

For the present we would ask you to treat this information as strictly confidential.

Yours faithfully,
for EAGLE OIL & SHIPPING COMPANY LTD.

(a-71)

Some of the men who re-boarded the San Demetrio Jack is standing on the extreme left

Jarvis Bay

San Demetrio

Admiral Scheer

The damaged deck of the San Demetrio

These photographs clearly show how badly damaged the ship was

Holed just above the waterline